How to Draw Cute Endangered Animals

For Kids & Beginning Artists

Spencer G. Hale

Note to Parents:

All children are artists.
A child listens and learns best when they are quietly creating and having fun.
Encouragement and praise are the best things you can do for your budding artist.
A child may become a great artist if they have the following 5 things:
- Encouragement,
- Desire,
- Determination,
- Practice, and
- Patience.

'FUN FACTS' are included to educate and entertain while they draw.

Drawing Instructions:

1. **Draw wherever you would like** – at a desk, on the floor, on your bed, on the couch, or wherever you feel comfortable.
2. **Things you will need** – pencil, eraser, and paper. And maybe a pen, marker or crayons.
3. **Follow the instructions** for each animal by drawing over the larger image on the right, as a guide . Or **do it your own way on a large drawing pad**, and adding, subtracting, or changing whatever you would like.
4. Start by **Drawing Lightly** with a pencil so you can easily **Erase.**
5. **Be Bold** - Try drawing large and bold to fill most of the page. But remember to draw lightly.
6. And Finally, when the drawing is complete, **draw over your light lines with darker lines** using a pencil, pen, marker, or crayons.
7. **Enjoy coloring** your newly finished drawing. Be creative with your colors.
8. **Most of all** - enjoy yourself, have fun, and show-off your new drawing to everyone.
9. **Practice** - Don't worry about drawing perfectly at first, You will get better as you practice a lot.

The Art of Cute

Here are some fun ways to make an animal look cute:
Head and Body - Draw the head larger and body smaller.
Eyes - Draw bigger eyes, and/or draw them lower on the head.
Mouth - Draw your animal with a smile.
Body - Draw larger hands, paws, claws, feet, and hooves, in comparison to the rest of the body.

Now, when you've had some practice, let's do something really fun:
Using all of these drawing tricks, create your own Cute Animal drawing from a photo, a painting, or from a live animal.

Thanks for buying my book!

If you find this book fun and helpful, I will be grateful
if you would write a raving review on Amazon.

Your reviews make a huge difference, and I personally read every one.

If you would like to leave a review, go to the Amazon
page for this book and click "Write a customer review".

Thank you so much.

Spencer G. Hale

Fun Animals to Draw

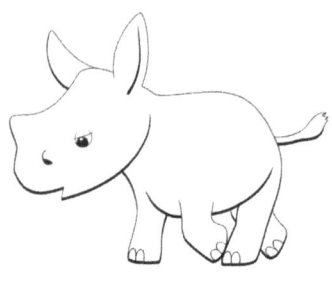

White Rhino Baby

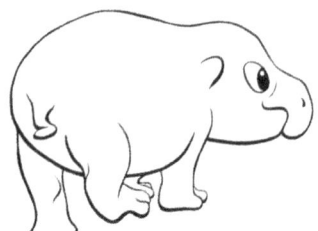

Pygmy Hippo

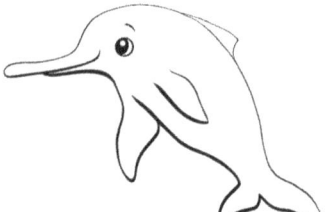

Baiji River Dolphine

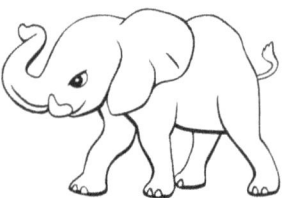

African Elephant

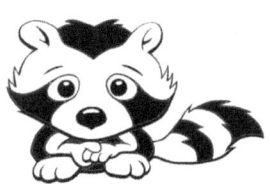

Cozumel Raccoon

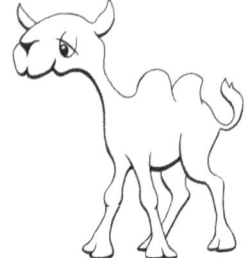

Bactrian Camel

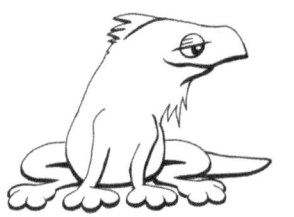

Galapagas Pink Land Iguana

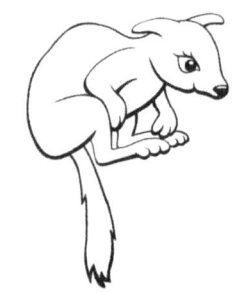

Golden Manted Tree Kangaroo

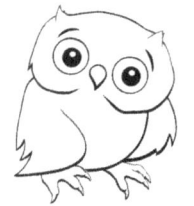

Pernambuco Pygmy Owl

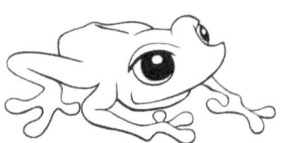

Golden Poison Dart Frog

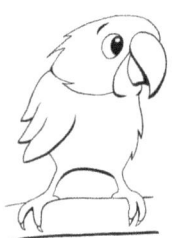

Glaucos Macaw

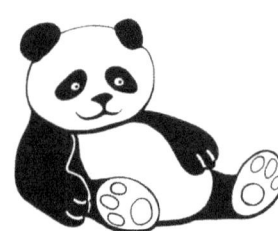

Giant Panda

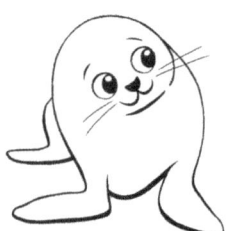

Hawaiian Monk Seal

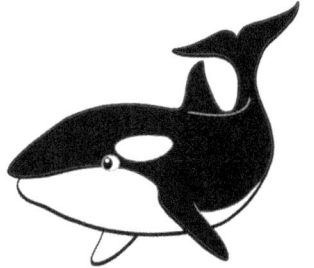

Orca

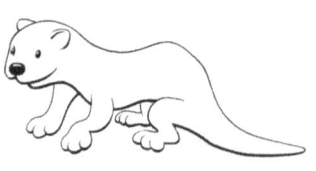

California Sea Otter

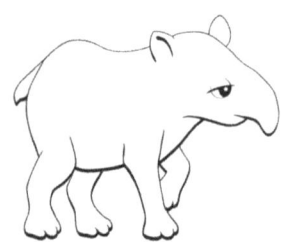

Central American Tapir

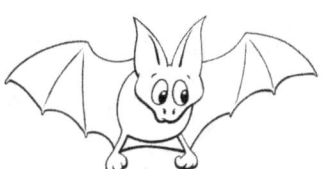

Sardinian Long-eared Bat

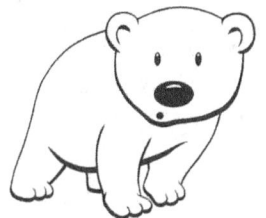

Polar Bear

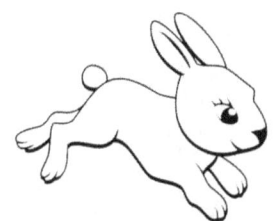

Riverine Rabbit

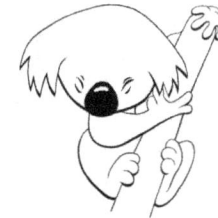

Koala

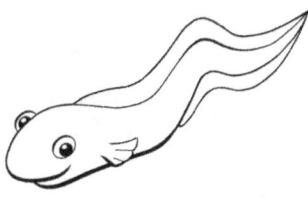

European Eel

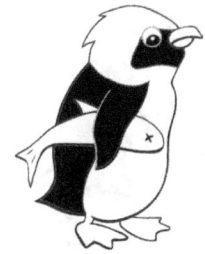

African Penguin

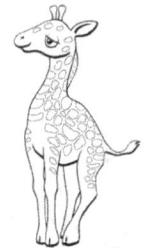

Nubian Giraffe

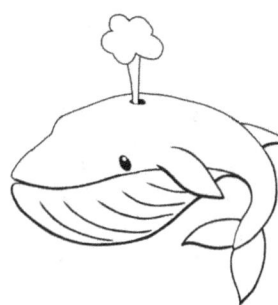

Blue Whale

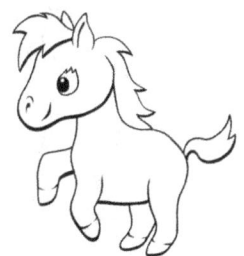

Przewalski's Horse

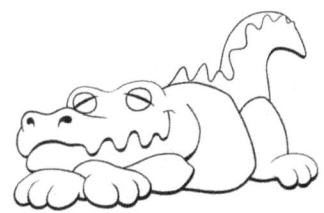

Philippine crocodile

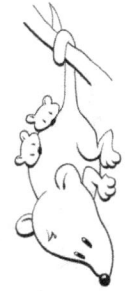

Mountain Pygmy Opposum

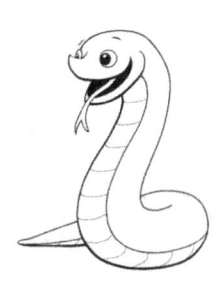

Southern Hog-nosed Snake

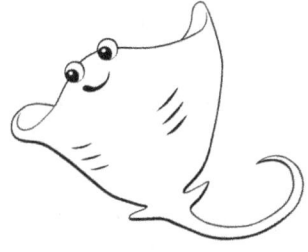

Giant Freshwater Stingray

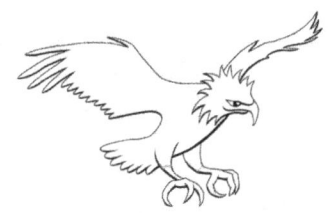

Philippine Eagle

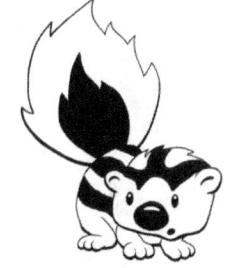

Eastern Spotted Skunk

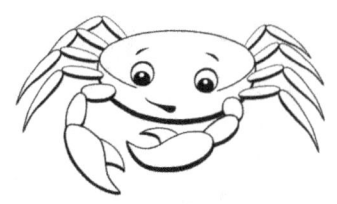

Giri Putri Cave Crab

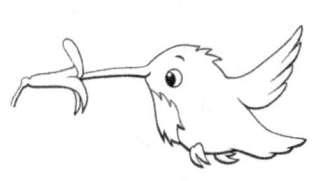

Gorgeted Puffleg Hummingbird

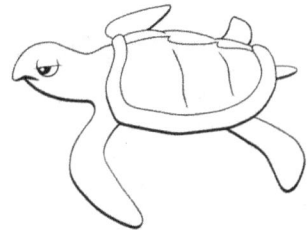

Kemp Ridley's Sea Turtle

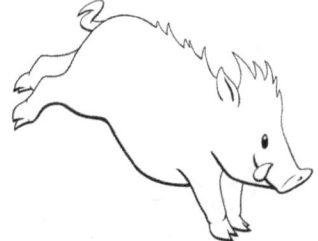

Visayan Warty Pig

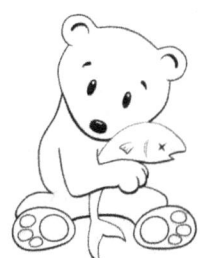

Asiatic Black Bear

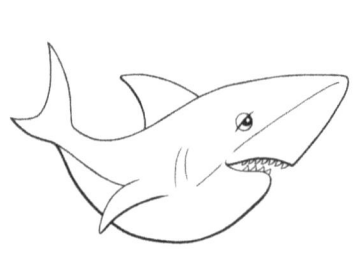

Great White Shark

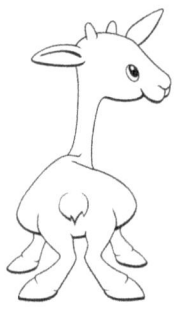

Arapawa Goat

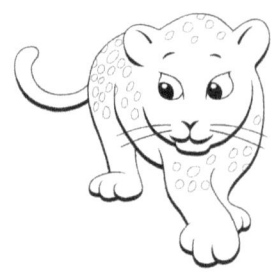

Amure Leopard Cub

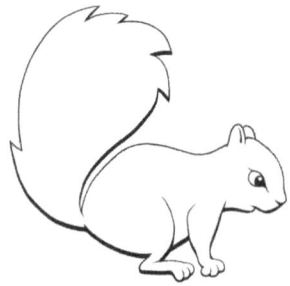

Western Gray Squirrel

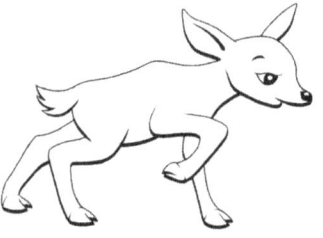

Key Deer

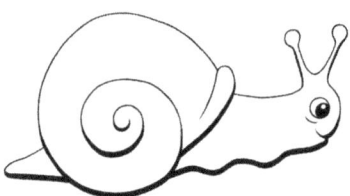

Poweiiiphanta Snail

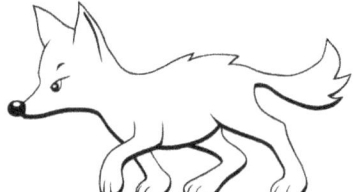

Sierra Nevada Gray Fox

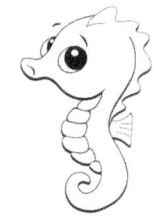

Cape Seahorse

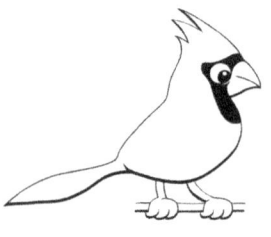

Yellow Cardinal

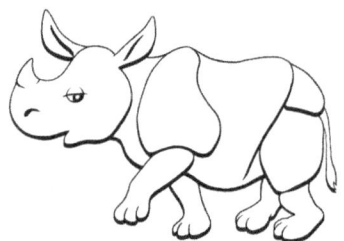

Javan Rhinoceros

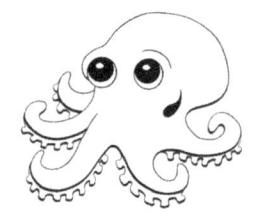

Cirroctopus hochbergi Octopus

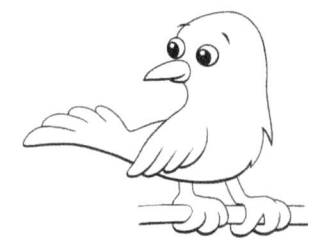

Pinyan Jay

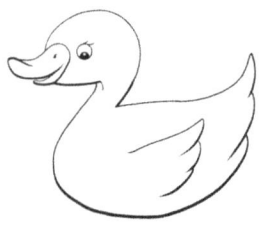

Madagascar Pochard Duck

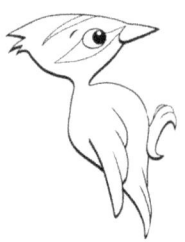

Ivory Billed Woodpecker

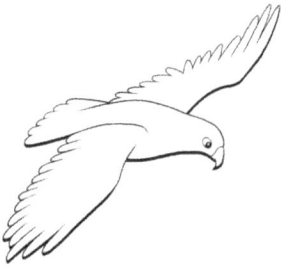

Ridgway's Hawk

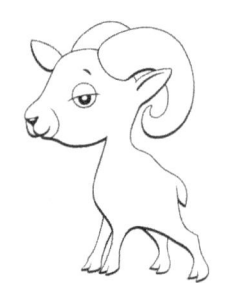

Peninsular Bighorn Sheep

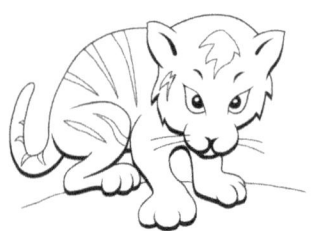

Amur Tiger Cub

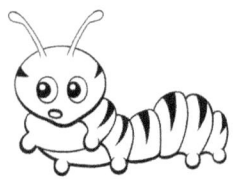

Monarch Caterpillar

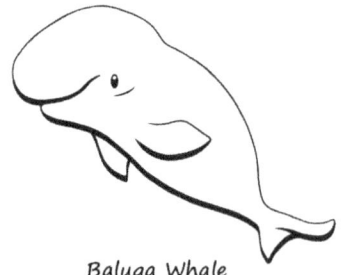

Baluga Whale

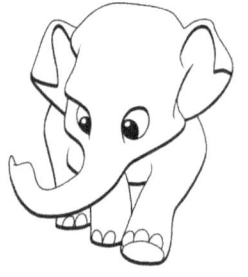

Baby Asian Elephant

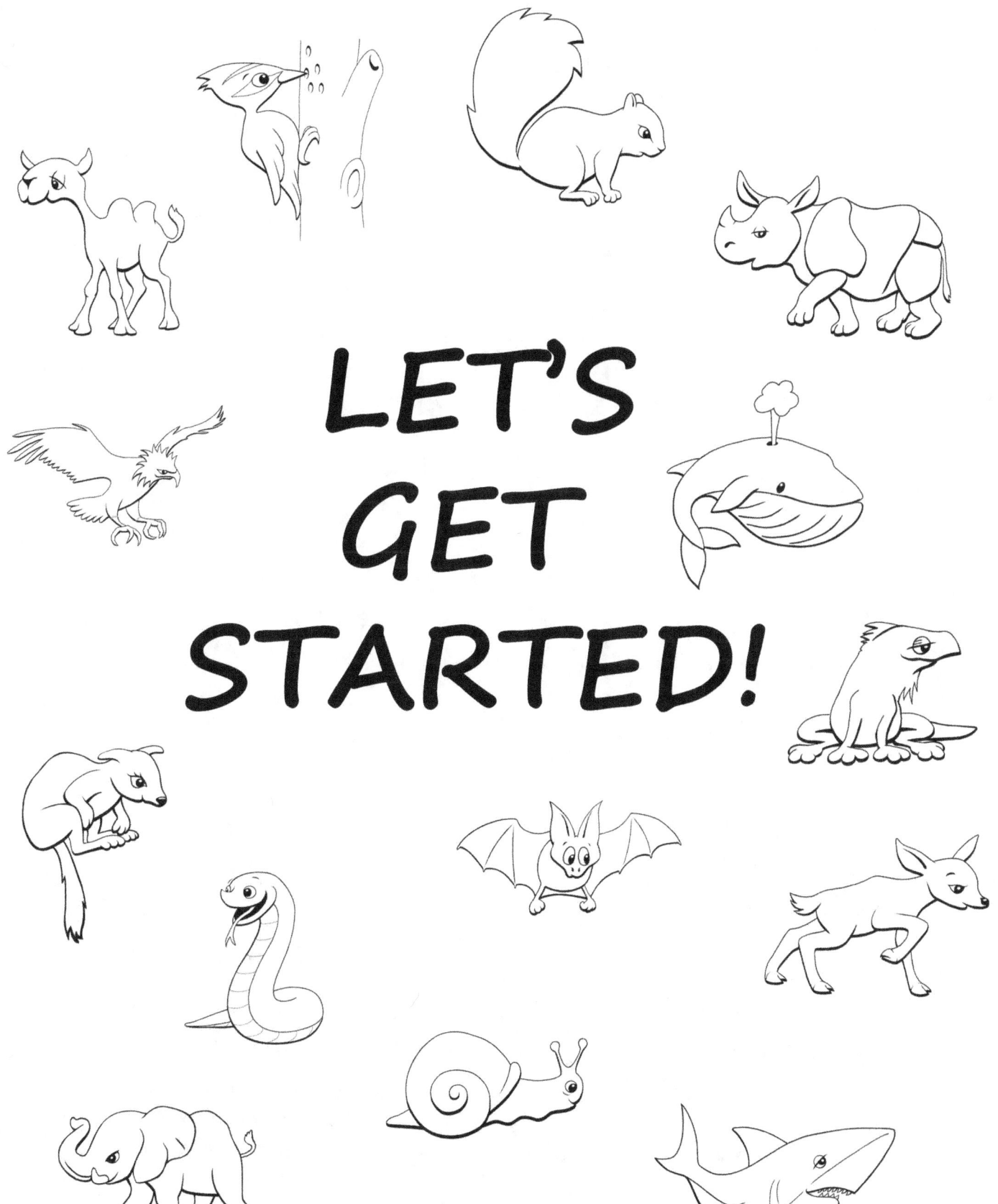

LET'S
GET
STARTED!

STEP 2: Draw light lines

STEP 3: Erase the circles

STEP 4 - FINISH:
Add details, Draw dark

DRAWING TIPS:

Try drawing some lines thick,
and other lines thin.

Try drawing different shaped eyes

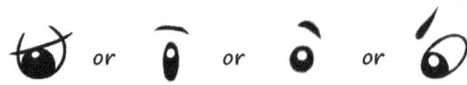

Baby White Rhino

Use this as a guide for each of the steps in creating your own drawing.

Fun Facts:

White Rhino

Reasons for Endangerment:
1. Poaching: They are often illegally hunted for their horns, which some people wrongly believe have special powers.
2. Habitat Loss: Their living space in grasslands and savannas is being taken over for farming or building.
3. Climate Change: Changes in the climate can affect their food supply and the health of their habitats.

Population in the Wild:
• Around 18,000, with most being the Southern white rhino.
  The Northern white rhino is critically endangered with only a few individuals left.

Population in Captivity:
• Found in some wildlife sanctuaries, but they breed better in their natural habitat.

Countries/Areas of Natural Habitat:
• Mainly found in southern African countries like South Africa, Namibia, Zimbabwe, and Kenya.

Interesting Facts:
1. Grass Grazers: They have wide mouths that are perfect for eating lots of grass.
2. Big and Heavy: They are the second-largest land mammal after the elephant, and can weigh over 2,000 kilograms (about 4,400 pounds).
3. Social Animals: White rhinos can be quite social.
   They sometimes hang out in groups, especially mothers with their babies or young adult females.

STEP 1 - START:
Draw light circles

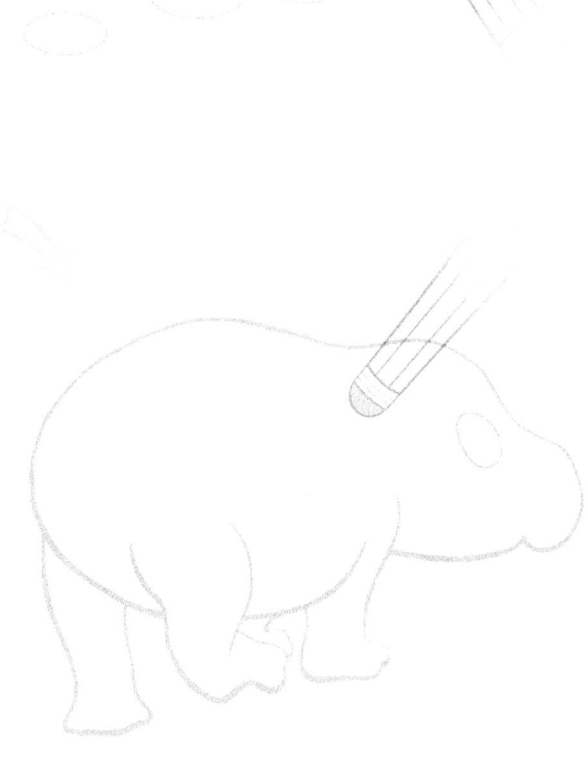

STEP 2: Draw light lines

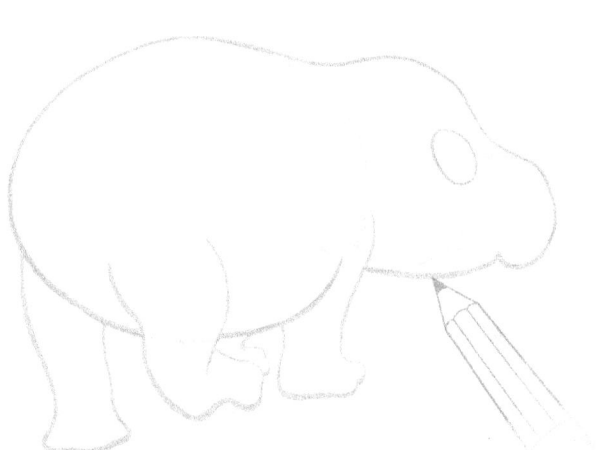

STEP 3: Erase the circles

STEP 4 - FINISH:
Add details, Draw dark

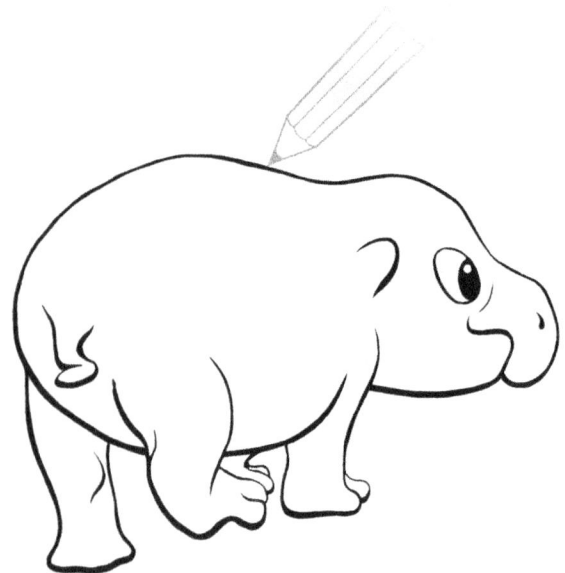

DRAWING TIPS:

Try drawing some lines thick,
and other lines thin.

Try drawing different shaped eyes

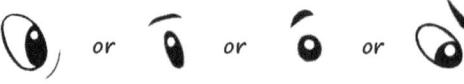

Pygmy Hippo

Use this as a guide for each of the steps in creating your own drawing.

Fun Facts:

Pygmy Hippo

Reasons for Endangerment:
1. Habitat Loss: Their homes in the forests and wetlands are being destroyed for logging and to make farms.
2. Hunting: Some people hunt them for their meat or because they think the pygmy hippos are pests.
3. Water Pollution: The water where they live can get polluted, which makes it hard for them to find clean food and water.

Population in the Wild:
• Estimated to be less than 3,000, but it's hard to know for sure because they are shy and live in dense forests.

Population in Captivity:
• A number are kept in zoos around the world, where breeding programs help to protect them.

Countries/Areas of Natural Habitat:
• Found in West Africa, mainly in countries like Liberia, Sierra Leone, Guinea, and Ivory Coast.

Interesting Facts:
1. Shy and Solitary: Unlike their larger cousins, pygmy hippos are very shy and usually live alone or with just a few others.
2. Nighttime Foragers: They are nocturnal, which means they are most active at night, spending their time searching for food like leaves, roots, and fruits.
3. Water Lovers: They spend a lot of time in water, which helps keep their skin cool and moist. They even have special valves in their ears and nostrils that close when they go underwater!

STEP 1 – START:
Draw light circles

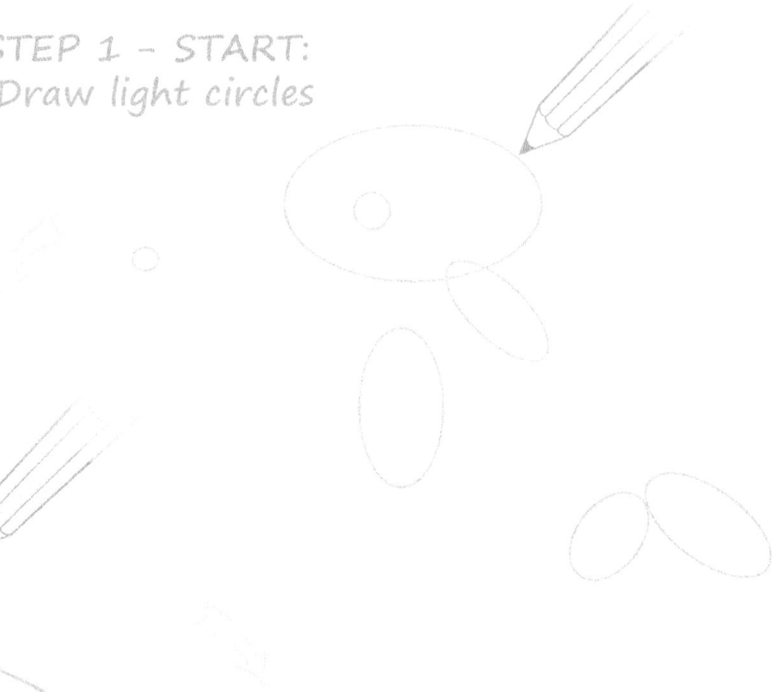

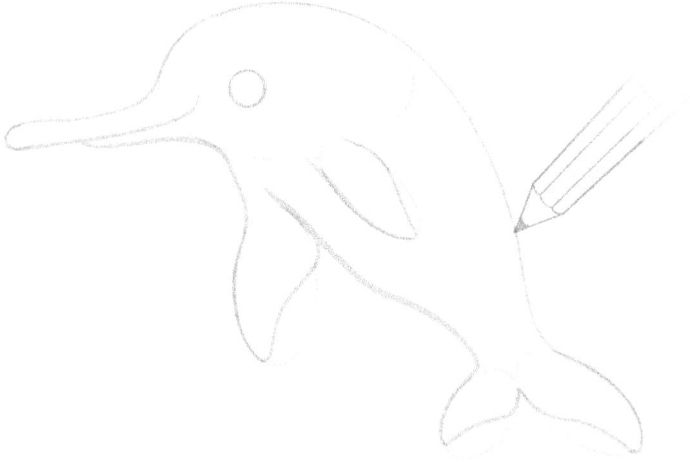

STEP 2: Draw light lines

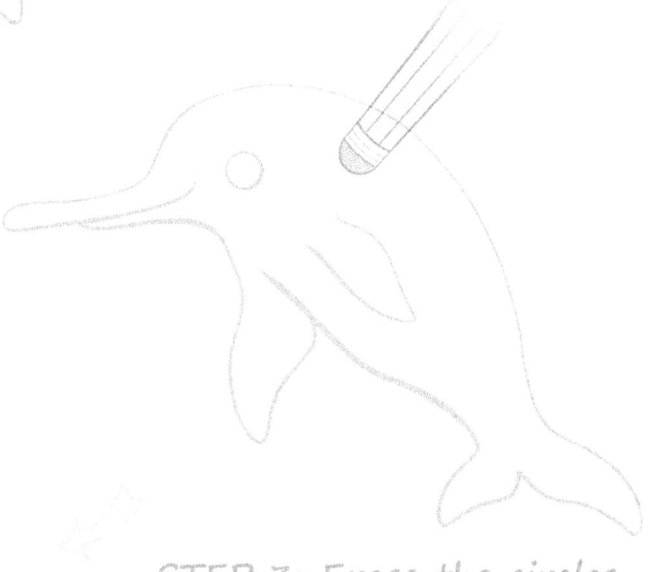

STEP 3: Erase the circles

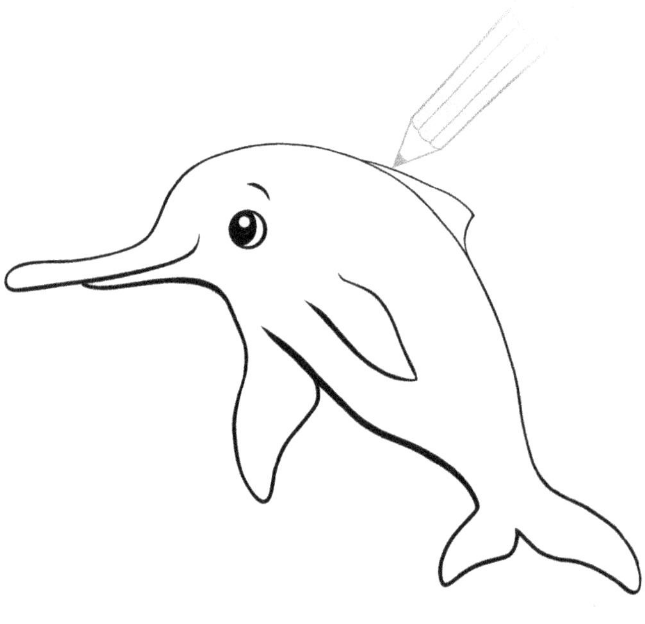

STEP 4 – FINISH:
Add details, Draw dark

DRAWING TIPS:

Try drawing some lines thick,
and other lines thin.

Try drawing different shaped eyes

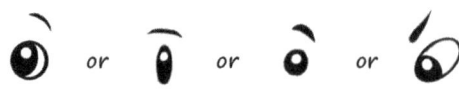 or ... or ... or ...

Baiji River Dolphin

Use this as a guide for each of the steps in creating your own drawing.

Fun Facts:

Baiji River Dolphin

Reasons for Endangerment:
1. Habitat Pollution: Their home in the Yangtze River got very polluted with chemicals and waste from factories and farms.
2. Boat Traffic: Lots of boats on the river made it noisy and dangerous for the dolphins, and sometimes they would get hurt by the boats.
3. Fishing Nets: They often got caught in nets that people used for fishing, which made it hard for them to swim and find food.

Population in the Wild:
• Possibly extinct. The last confirmed sighting was in 2002, and extensive searches since then have not found any baiji dolphins.

Population in Captivity:
• There were a few attempts to keep them in captivity, but they didn't survive long, and there are currently none in captivity.

Countries/Areas of Natural Habitat:
• They lived only in the Yangtze River in China.

Interesting Facts:
1. Nicknamed 'Goddess of the Yangtze': The baiji river dolphin was an important part of Chinese culture and was considered a goddess by some local people.
2. Echolocation Experts: Like other dolphins, they used echolocation to navigate and find food in the murky waters of the Yangtze River.
3. Very Rare: Even before they became so endangered, baiji river dolphins were one of the rarest and most ancient types of dolphins.

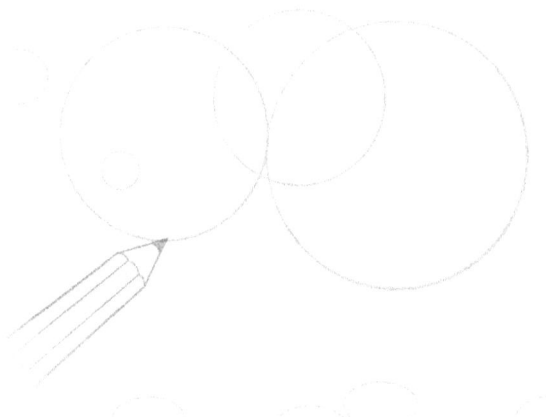

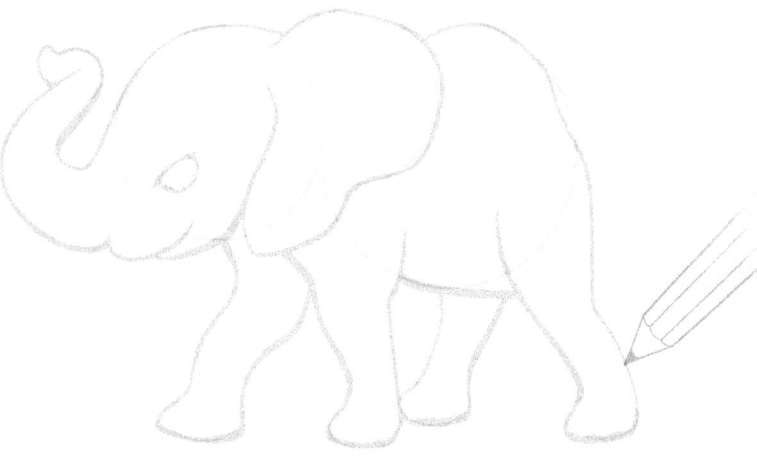

STEP 2: Draw light lines

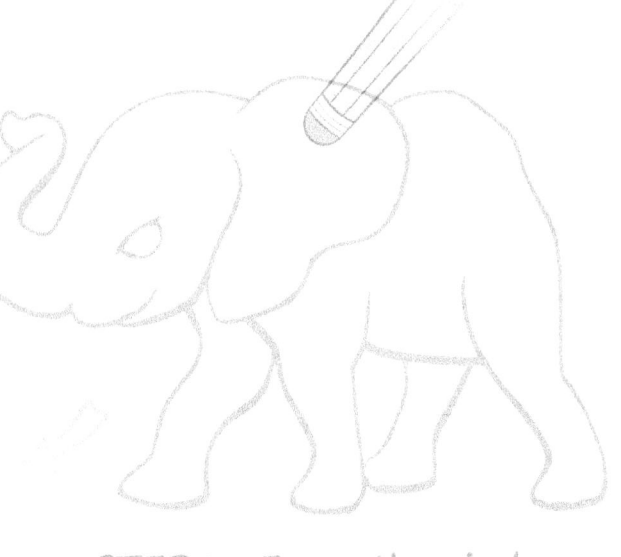

STEP 3: Erase the circles

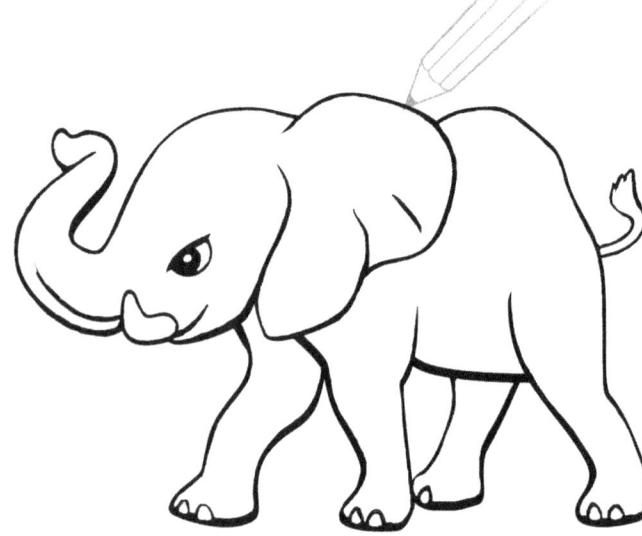

STEP 4 - FINISH:
Add details, Draw dark

DRAWING TIPS:

Try drawing some lines thick,
and other lines thin.

Try drawing different shaped eyes

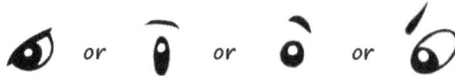

Baby African Elephant

Use this as a guide for each of the steps in creating your own drawing.

Fun Facts:

African Elephant

Reasons for Endangerment:
1. Poaching: They are often hunted illegally for their ivory tusks, which are highly valued in some cultures.
2. Habitat Loss: Their natural habitats, like savannas and forests, are being converted into farmland or used for human settlement.
3. Human-Elephant Conflict: As their living space becomes smaller, they sometimes enter farms to eat crops, leading to conflicts with farmers.

Population in the Wild:
• Estimated to be around 415,000, but their numbers are decreasing due to threats like poaching and habitat loss.

Population in Captivity:
• Some are found in zoos or wildlife parks, and others are protected in wildlife reserves and sanctuaries.

Countries/Areas of Natural Habitat:
• Found throughout sub-Saharan Africa, in countries like Kenya, Tanzania, Botswana, Zimbabwe, and South Africa, usually in savannas, grasslands, and forests.

Interesting Facts:
1. Largest Land Animal: They are the largest land animals on Earth, with their big ears and long tusks making them easy to recognize.
2. Social Creatures: They live in tight-knit family groups led by a female, called a matriarch, and they communicate with each other using sounds that humans can't hear.
3. Gardeners of the Savanna: By knocking down trees and eating plants, they help shape their environment, which creates habitats for other species.

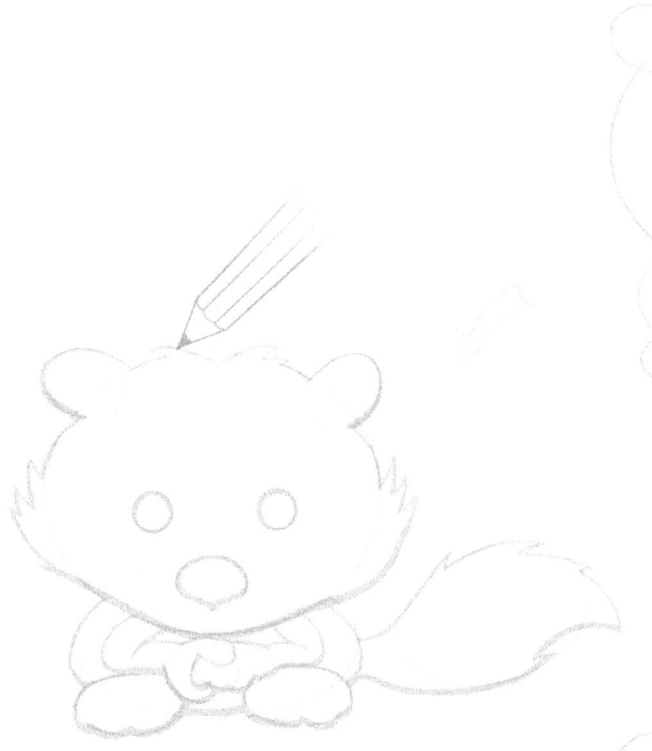

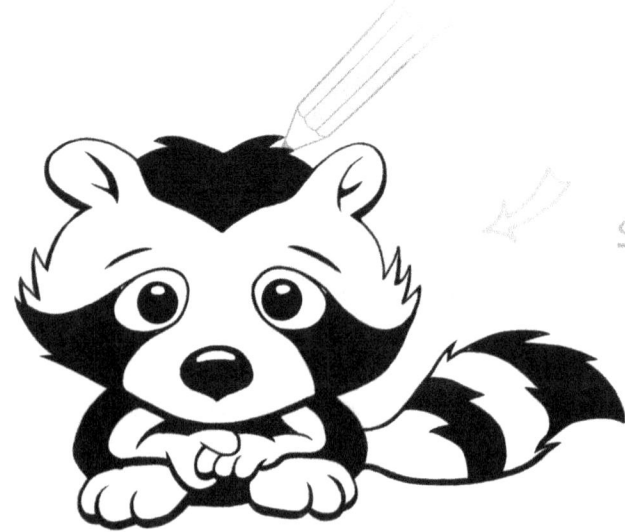

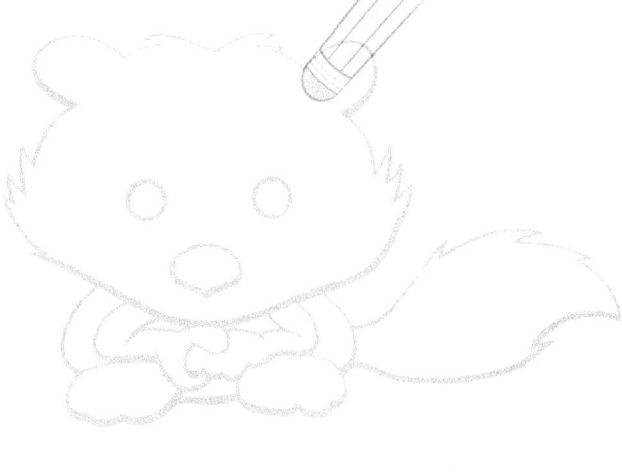

STEP 3: Erase the circles

DRAWING TIPS:

Try drawing some lines thick, and other lines thin.

Try drawing different shaped eyes

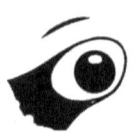 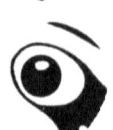 or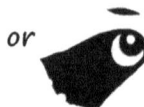

STEP 4 - FINISH:
Add details, Draw dark

Cozumel Pygmy Raccoon

Use this as a guide for each of the steps in creating your own drawing.

Fun Facts:

Cozumel Pygmy Raccoon

Reasons for Endangerment:
1. Habitat Loss: Their home on Cozumel Island is being changed due to building and development, leaving them with less space to live.
2. Disease: Diseases from domestic animals and other raccoons can spread to them and make them sick.
3. Limited Range: Since they only live on one small island, any changes to their environment can have a big impact on their population.

Population in the Wild:
• Very few, considered to be one of the most endangered types of raccoon.

Population in Captivity:
• Rarely found in captivity, efforts are mainly focused on protecting them in their natural habitat.

Countries/Areas of Natural Habitat:
• Found only on Cozumel Island, off the coast of the Yucatan Peninsula in Mexico.

Interesting Facts:
1. Unique Diet: They mainly eat crabs, which makes them different from other raccoons that eat a variety of foods.
2. Nocturnal Animals: They are active at night, spending the night looking for food and resting during the day.
3. Swimming Skills: They are good swimmers and can swim between different parts of their island home.

STEP 1 – START:
Draw light circles

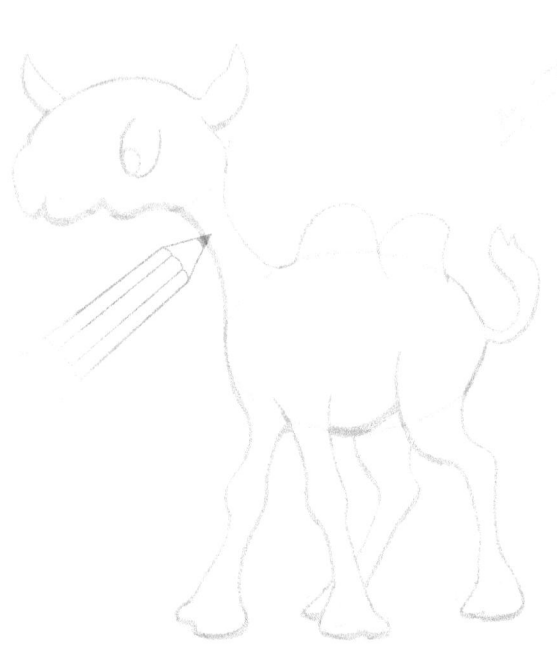

STEP 2: Draw light lines

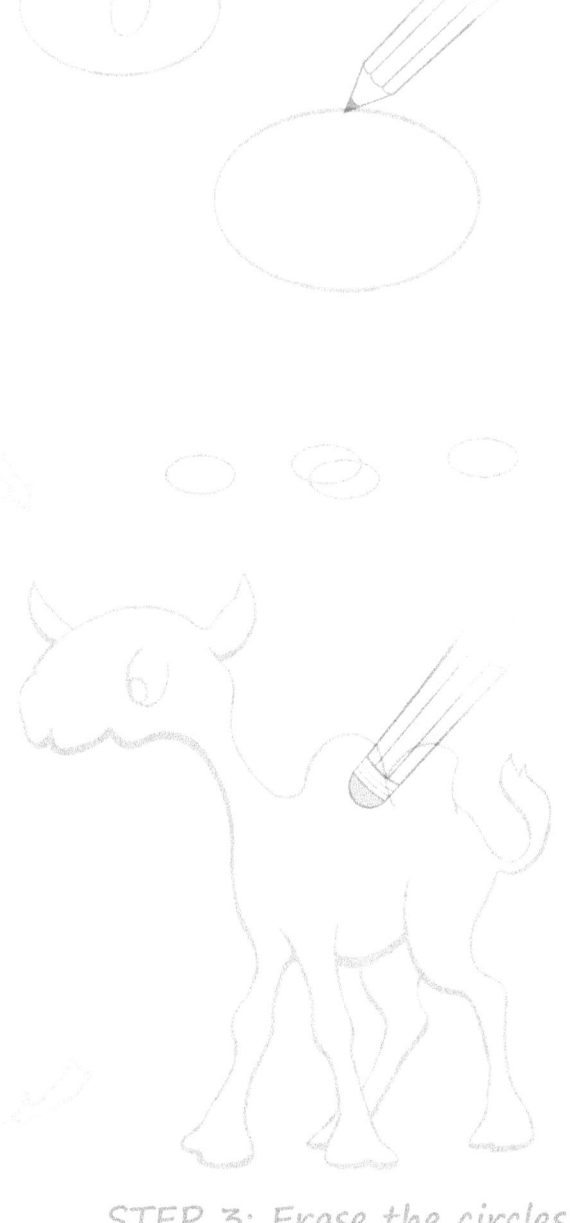

STEP 3: Erase the circles

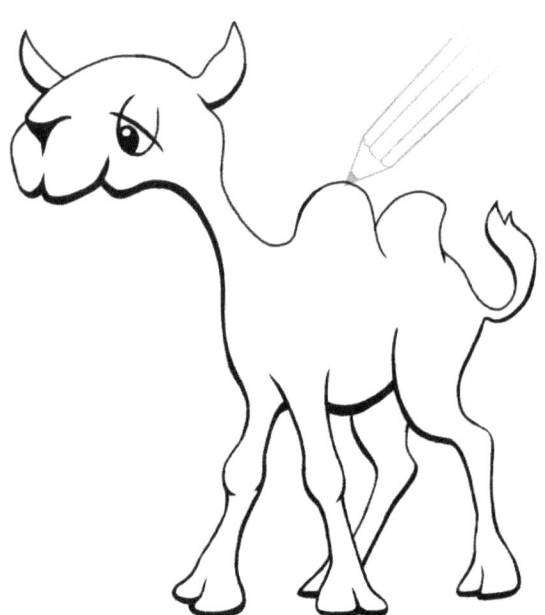

STEP 4 – FINISH:
Add details, Draw dark

DRAWING TIPS:

Try drawing some lines thick,
and other lines thin.

Try drawing different shaped eyes

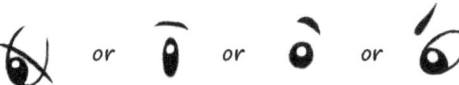

Bactrian Camel

Use this as a guide
for each of the
steps in creating
your own drawing.

Fun Facts:

Bactrian Camel

Reasons for Endangerment:
1. Habitat Loss: Places where they live are being used for mining and farming, which takes away their space and food.
2. Competition for Water: They have to share their water sources with people and other animals, which sometimes leaves not enough for them.
3. Hunting: Some people hunt them for their meat and fur, even though it's not allowed.

Population in the Wild:
• Very few, estimated to be around 600 to 1,000 wild Bactrian camels left.

Population in Captivity:
• Many live in zoos and nature reserves, and there are also domesticated Bactrian camels used by people in their native regions.

Countries/Areas of Natural Habitat:
• Found in the Gobi Desert in Mongolia and some parts of China.

Interesting Facts:
1. Two Humps: Unlike their one-humped cousins (dromedary camels), Bactrian camels have two humps, which store fat that can be converted into energy when food is scarce.
2. Built for the Desert: They can drink up to 30 gallons of water at once and can survive in extreme temperatures, from freezing cold to blistering heat.
3. Tough Feet: Their large, flat feet are adapted to walking in the desert, helping them move easily over sand without sinking.

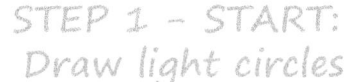

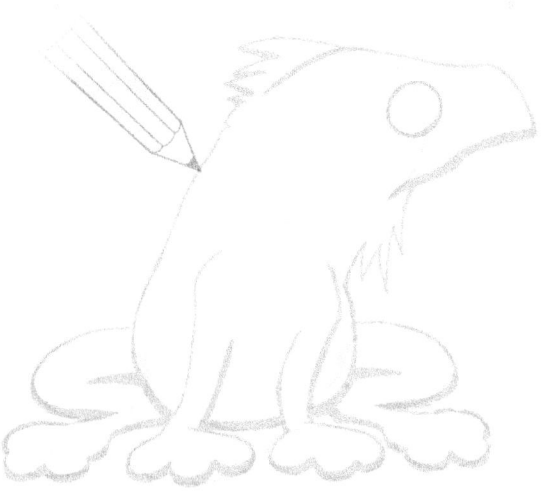

STEP 2: Draw light lines

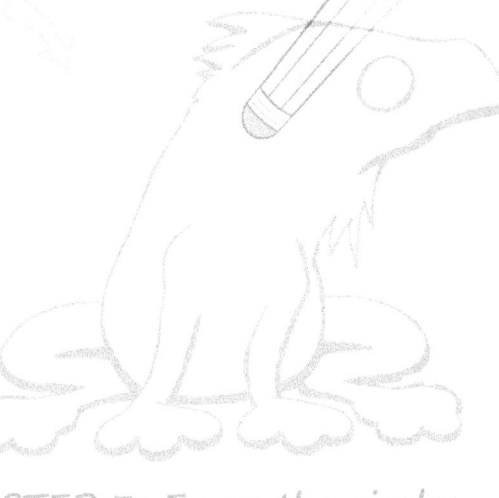

STEP 3: Erase the circles

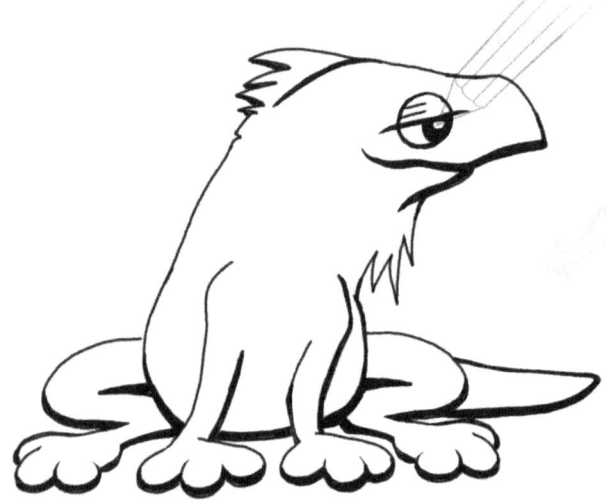

STEP 4 – FINISH:
Add details, Draw dark

DRAWING TIPS:

Try drawing some lines thick,
and other lines thin.

Try drawing different shaped eyes

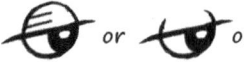 or or or

Galapagas Pink Land Iguana

Use this as a guide
for each of the
steps in creating
your own drawing.

Fun Facts:

Galapagos Pink Land Iguana

Reasons for Endangerment:
1. Limited Habitat: They live in a very small area, so any changes or damage to their habitat can have a big impact on their population.
2. Invasive Species: Animals brought to the islands, like goats, can eat the plants the iguanas need for food.
3. Climate Change: Changes in climate can affect their food sources and the overall health of their habitat.

Population in the Wild:
• Very few, estimated to be around 200 individuals.

Population in Captivity:
• Not typically kept in captivity due to the focus on preserving their natural habitat and strict conservation laws.

Countries/Areas of Natural Habitat:
• Found only on Isabela Island in the Galapagos Islands, Ecuador.

Interesting Facts:
1. Unique Color: They are the only iguanas in the world with a pink color, mixed with some dark stripes.
2. Late Discovery: They were only officially recognized as a separate species in 2009, making them one of the newest species of iguana to be identified.
3. Volcanic Dwellers: They primarily live on and around the Wolf Volcano, one of the most active volcanoes in the Galapagos.

STEP 1 - START:
Draw light circles

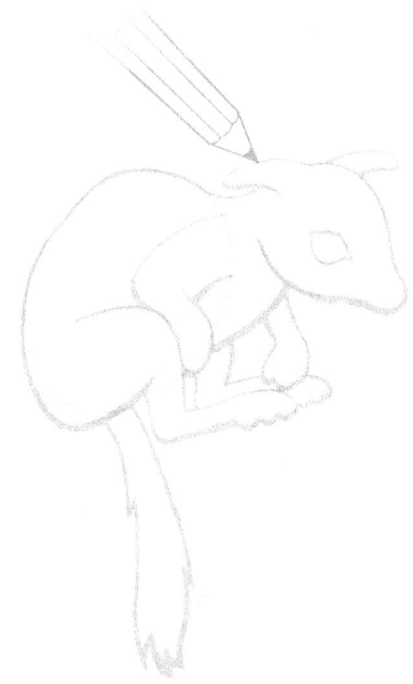

STEP 2: Draw light lines

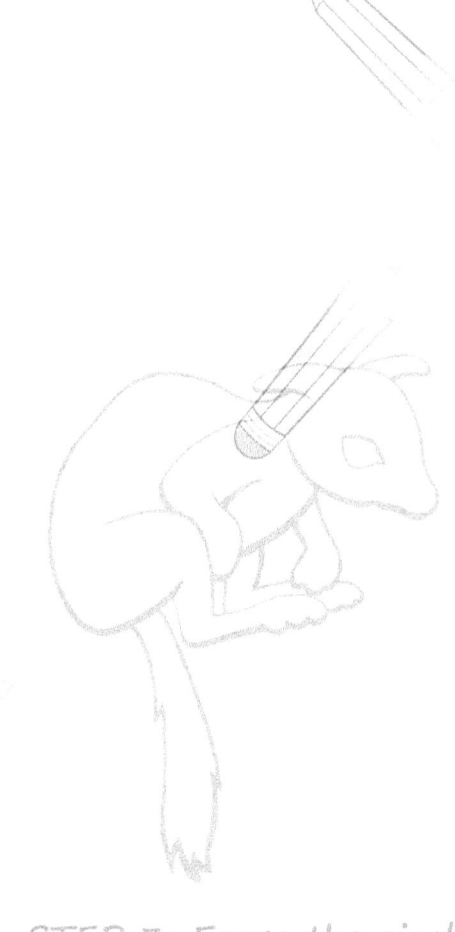

STEP 3: Erase the circles

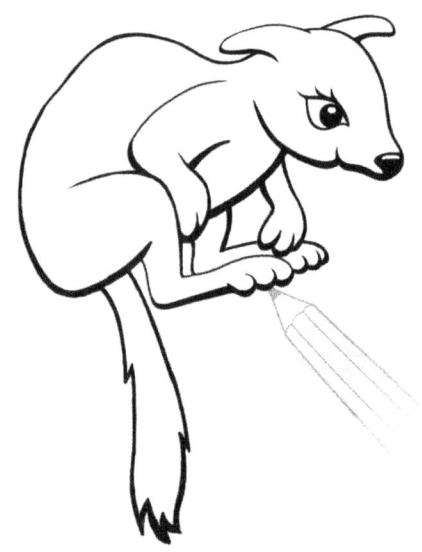

STEP 4 - FINISH:
Add details, Draw dark

DRAWING TIPS:

Try drawing some lines thick, and other lines thin.

Try drawing different shaped eyes

 or or or

Golden-Manted Tree Kangaroo

Use this as a guide for each of the steps in creating your own drawing.

Fun Facts:

Golden-Mantled Tree Kangaroo

Reasons for Endangerment:
  1. Habitat Loss: Their home in the rainforest is being cut down for timber and to make space for farming.
  2. Hunting: Some people hunt them for food and their fur, even though it's not allowed.
  3. Climate Change: Changes in the climate can affect their habitat and the availability of their food sources.
Population in the Wild:
  • Not precisely known, but they are considered to be a rare species.
Population in Captivity:
  • Very few in captivity, mostly found in conservation programs and zoos.
Countries/Areas of Natural Habitat:
  • Found in the mountainous rainforests of Papua New Guinea.
Interesting Facts:
  1. Amazing Climbers: Unlike their ground-dwelling relatives, tree kangaroos are adapted to life in the trees with strong forelimbs for climbing.
  2. Unique Diet: They mostly eat leaves and fruit, and have a stomach that's similar to a cow's to help them digest all the plant material.
  3. Slow and Steady: They move carefully and slowly through the trees but can leap to the ground from high up without getting hurt.

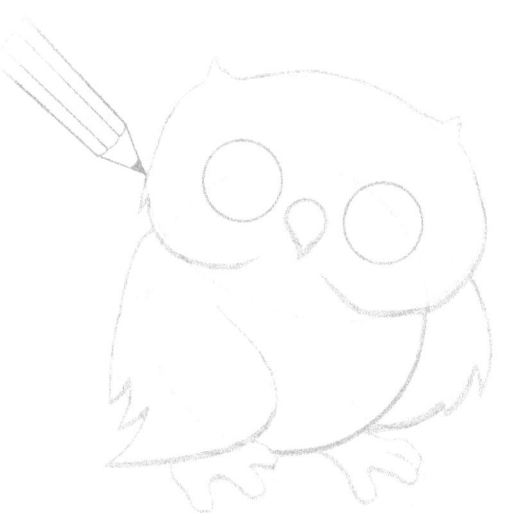

STEP 2: Draw light lines

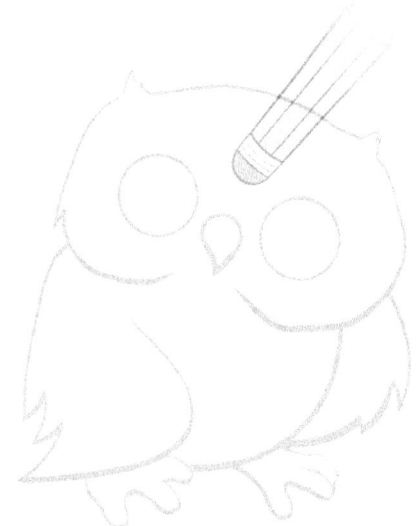

STEP 3: Erase the circles

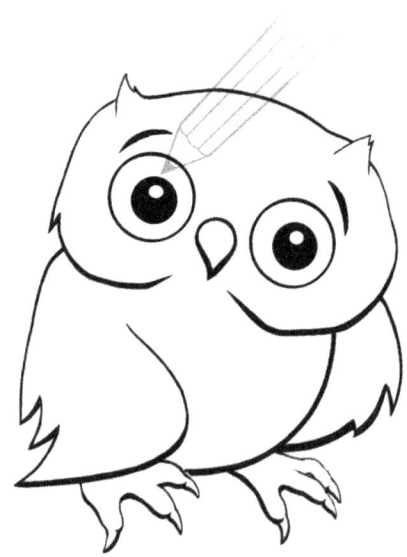

STEP 4 - FINISH:
Add details, Draw dark

DRAWING TIPS:

Try drawing some lines thick,
and other lines thin.

Try drawing different shaped eyes

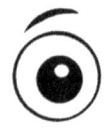 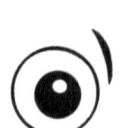 or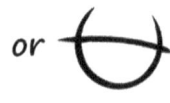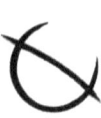

Pernambuco Pygmy Owl

Use this as a guide
for each of the
steps in creating
your own drawing.

Fun Facts:

Pernambuco Pygmy Owl

Reasons for Endangerment:
1. Habitat Loss: Their homes in the forests are being cut down to use the land for farming or building houses.
2. Deforestation: The trees they live in and around are being cut down for wood, leaving them with fewer places to nest and hunt.
3. Pesticides: Chemicals used in farming can poison the small insects and animals they eat.

Population in the Wild:
• Not well-known, but they are considered very rare and are one of the most endangered owl species.

Population in Captivity:
• Rarely found in captivity, as they are a relatively recently discovered species and are challenging to breed outside of their natural habitat.

Countries/Areas of Natural Habitat:
• Found in a small area of northeastern Brazil, especially in the Atlantic Forest of Pernambuco.

Interesting Facts:
1. Nocturnal Hunters: Like most owls, they are active at night, using their excellent night vision and hearing to find food.
2. Small Size: They are very small owls, making them hard to spot in the wild.
3. Important for the Ecosystem: As predators of insects and small animals, they help control the population of these creatures and maintain a balanced ecosystem.

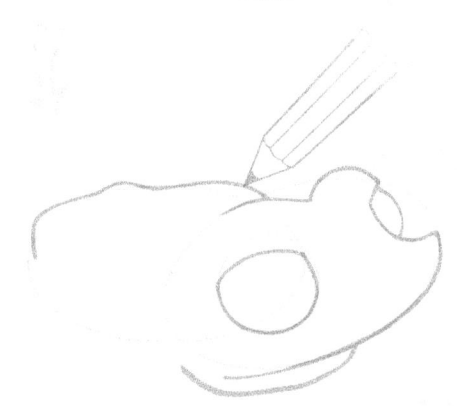

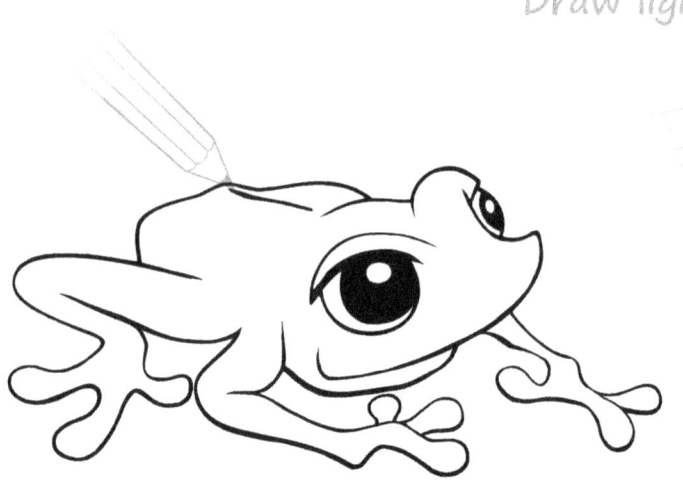

STEP 6 – FINISH:
Add details, Draw dark

STEP 2: Draw light lines

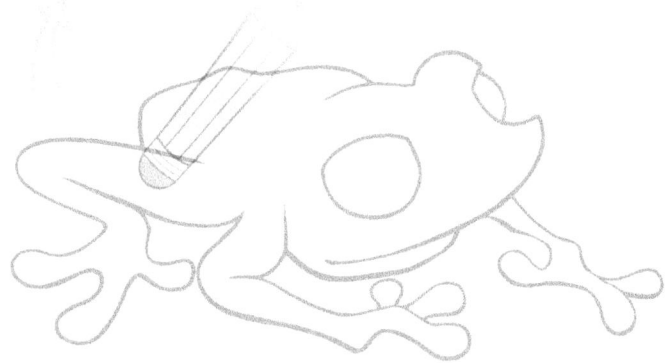

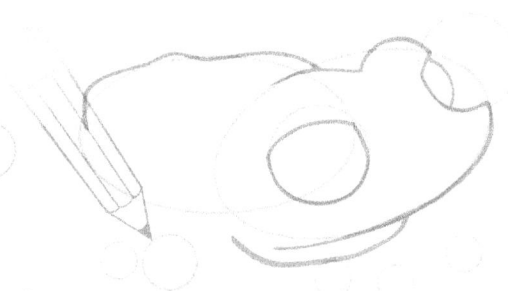

STEP 5: Erase the circles

STEP 3: Draw light circles
for feet and legs

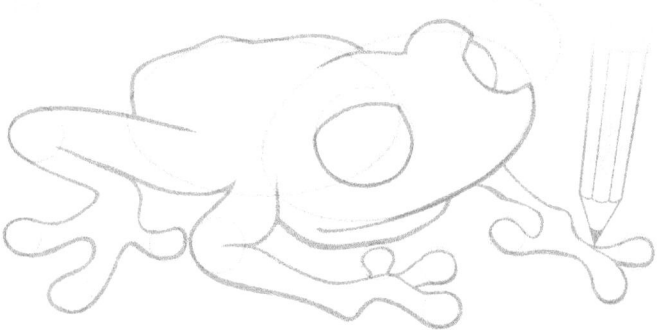

STEP 4: Draw light lines
for feet and legs

DRAWING TIPS:

Try drawing some lines thick,
and other lines thin.

Try drawing different shaped eyes

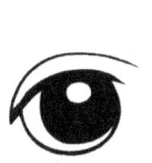 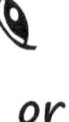 or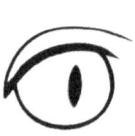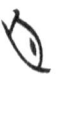

Golden Poison Dart Frog

Use this as a guide for each of the steps in creating your own drawing.

Fun Facts:

Golden Poison Dart Frog

Reasons for Endangerment:
  1. Habitat Loss: Their home in the rainforest is being destroyed for farming, logging, and mining.
  2. Pollution: Chemicals and waste from human activities can pollute their environment and make them sick.
  3. Collection for Pets: Some people catch them to keep as pets or use them to make traditional medicines.
Population in the Wild:
  • Not exactly known, but their numbers are believed to be decreasing.
Population in Captivity:
  • They are bred in captivity for conservation and are also kept in zoos and private collections.
Countries/Areas of Natural Habitat:
  • Found only in a small area of the Pacific coast of Colombia, in rainforests with high humidity.
Interesting Facts:
  1. Incredibly Poisonous: They are one of the most poisonous animals on Earth. Just touching them can be dangerous because of the toxin in their skin.
  2. Bright Warning Colors: Their bright golden color warns predators that they are poisonous and not a good idea to eat.
  3. Caring Parents: They lay their eggs on the ground, and when the eggs hatch, the parents carry the tadpoles on their back to water where they can grow into frogs.

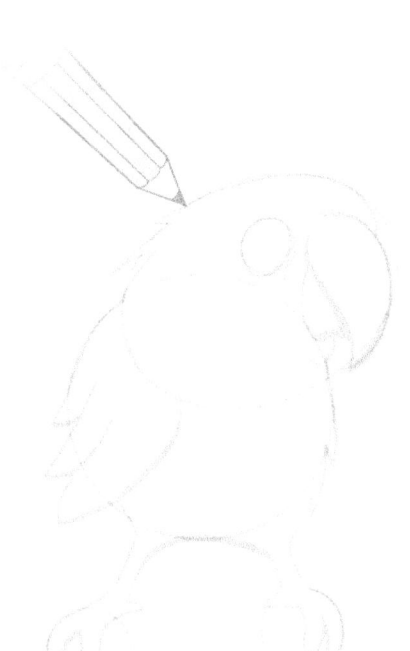

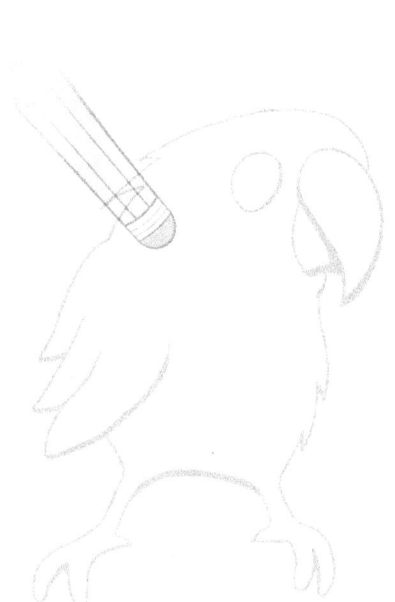

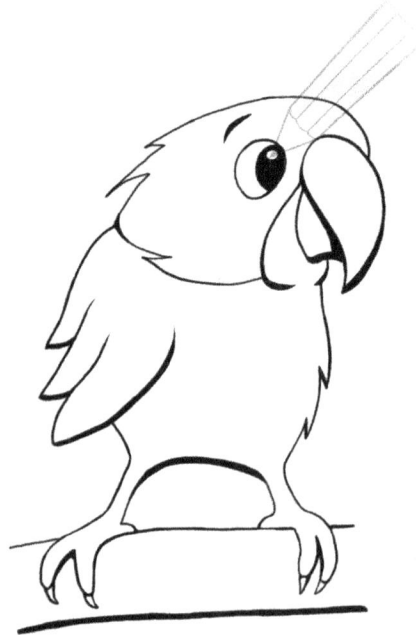

STEP 3: Erase the circles

STEP 4 – FINISH:
Add details, Draw dark

DRAWING TIPS:

Try drawing some lines thick,
and other lines thin.

Try drawing different shaped eyes

 or   or   or

Glaucos Macaw

Use this as a guide
for each of the
steps in creating
your own drawing.

Fun Facts:

Glaucous Macaw

Reasons for Endangerment:
   1. Habitat Loss: Their homes in the forests were cleared for farming and development.
   2. Trapping for Pet Trade: Many were captured to be sold as pets, which greatly reduced their numbers in the wild.
   3. Hunting: They were sometimes hunted for their feathers and for food.
Population in the Wild:
   • Believed to be extinct in the wild, with the last confirmed sightings in the 19th century.
Population in Captivity:
   • There are no known individuals in captivity. The species is considered extinct or critically endangered.
Countries/Areas of Natural Habitat:
   • Historically found in regions of Argentina, Uruguay, and Brazil, especially near rivers and in palm groves.
Interesting Facts:
   1. Beautiful Appearance: They had striking blue feathers with greyish heads, making them very distinctive.
   2. Diet: Their diet mainly consisted of nuts from native palm trees.
   3. Mystery Bird: Because they disappeared so long ago and were not well-documented, there are still many mysteries about their behavior and exact habitat preferences.

STEP 1 - START:
Draw light circles

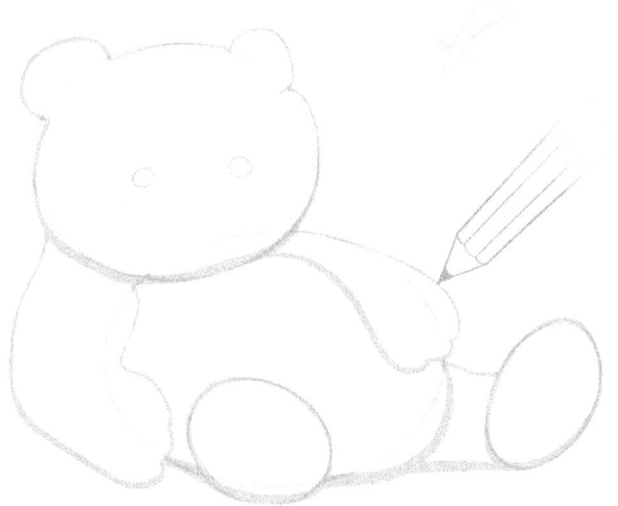

STEP 2: Draw light lines

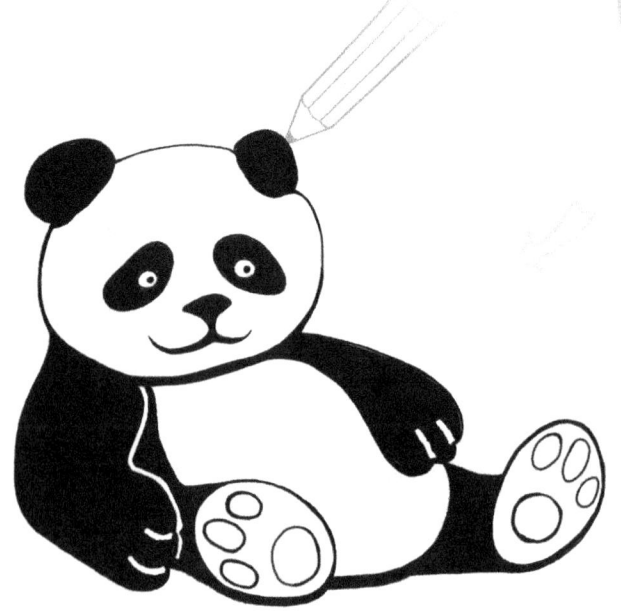

STEP 3: Erase the circles

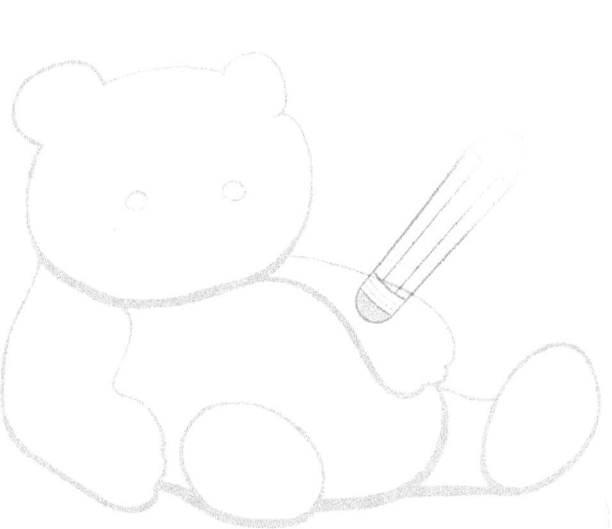

STEP 4 - FINISH:
Add details, Draw dark

DRAWING TIPS:

Try drawing some lines thick,
and other lines thin.

Try drawing different shaped eyes

  or

Giant Panda

Use this as a guide for each of the steps in creating your own drawing.

Fun Facts:

Giant Panda

Reasons for Endangerment:
1. Habitat Loss: Their bamboo forest homes are being cut down to make room for buildings and farms.
2. Low Birth Rate: They have a hard time having babies, and baby pandas are very small and fragile when they are born.
3. Bamboo Shortage: Sometimes the bamboo they eat dies off after blooming, which can leave them without enough food.

Population in the Wild:
- Around 1,800 to 2,000 in the wild, and their numbers have been increasing due to conservation efforts.

Population in Captivity:
- About 600 in zoos and breeding centers around the world, where they are part of programs to help increase their population.

Countries/Areas of Natural Habitat:
- Found in the mountain forests of central China, especially in Sichuan, Shaanxi, and Gansu provinces.

Interesting Facts:
1. Bamboo Buffet: They eat a lot of bamboo – up to 26 to 84 pounds of it a day – and they spend 12 to 16 hours a day just eating!
2. Black and White Fur: Their distinctive black and white fur helps them blend into the snowy and rocky environment of their habitat.
3. Great Climbers and Swimmers: Despite their bulky appearance, they are good at climbing trees and can swim very well.

STEP 1 – START:
Draw light circles

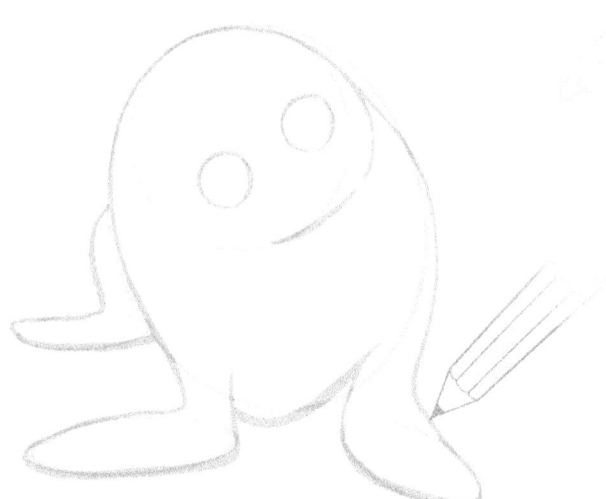

STEP 2: Draw light lines

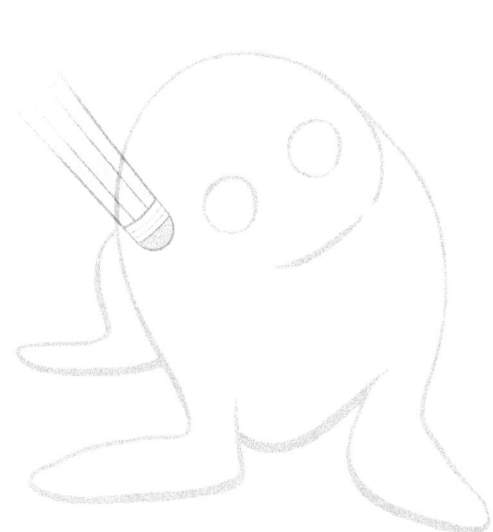

STEP 3: Erase the circles

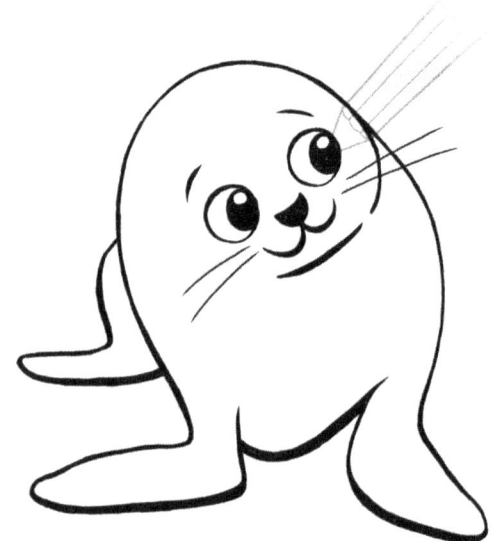

STEP 4 – FINISH:
Add details, Draw dark

DRAWING TIPS:

Try drawing some lines thick,
and other lines thin.

Try drawing different shaped eyes

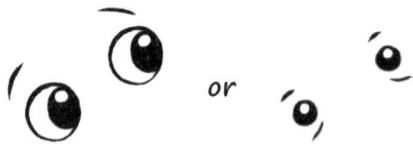

or

Hawaiian Monk Seal

Use this as a guide for each of the steps in creating your own drawing.

Fun Facts:

Hawaiian Monk Seal

Reasons for Endangerment:
1. Habitat Disturbance: Beaches where they rest and raise their pups are disturbed by human activities and development.
2. Food Shortage: Overfishing and changes in the ocean environment can make it hard for them to find enough food.
3. Entanglement in Debris: They can get caught in fishing nets or marine debris, which can hurt them or make it difficult for them to swim and find food.

Population in the Wild:
• Around 1,400, mostly living in the Northwestern Hawaiian Islands.

Population in Captivity:
• Very few in captivity, as efforts are focused on protecting and supporting them in their natural habitat.

Countries/Areas of Natural Habitat:
• Found only in the Hawaiian Islands, in the United States.

Interesting Facts:
1. Endemic Species: They are unique to Hawaii and can't be found anywhere else in the world.
2. Sunbathers: They enjoy resting on sandy beaches and volcanic rocks in between their long swims and dives.
3. Long Divers: They can hold their breath for up to 20 minutes and dive over 1,500 feet deep to find food on the ocean floor.

STEP 1 – START:
Draw light circles

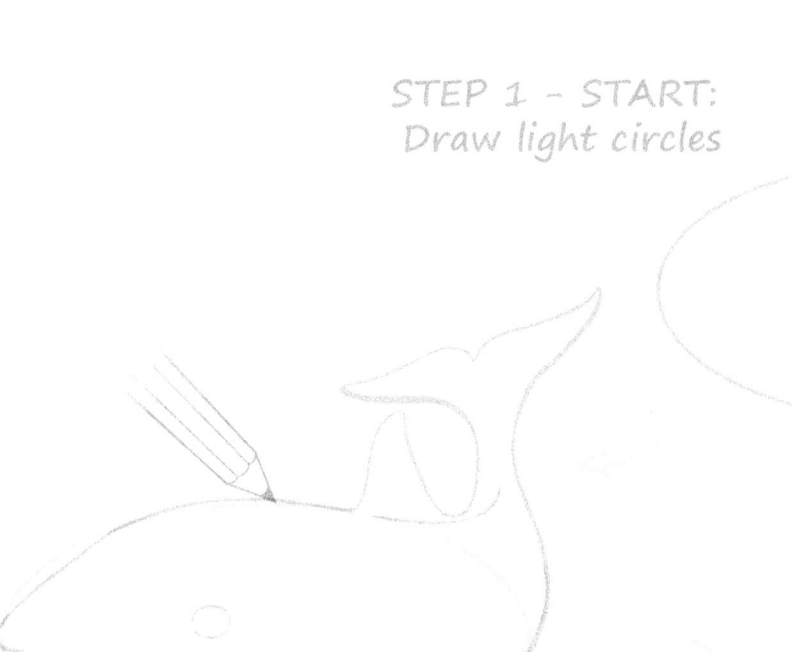

STEP 2: Draw light lines

STEP 3: Erase the circles

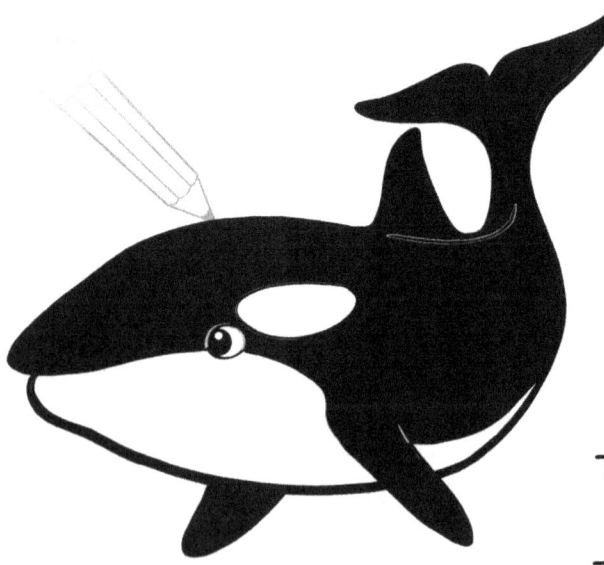

STEP 4 – FINISH:
Add details, Draw dark

DRAWING TIPS:

Try drawing some lines thick, and other lines thin.

Try drawing different shaped eyes

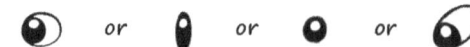

Orca

Use this as a guide
for each of the
steps in creating
your own drawing.

Fun Facts:

Orca (Killer Whale)

Reasons for Endangerment:
1. Pollution: Chemicals and waste in the ocean can contaminate their food and water, making them sick.
2. Overfishing: When there's less fish in the sea for them to eat, it can be hard for them to find enough food.
3. Noise Pollution: Noise from boats and other human activities can interfere with their communication and navigation.

Population in the Wild:
• Estimated to be around 50,000, but some specific populations, like the Southern Resident killer whales, are endangered and have much smaller numbers.

Population in Captivity:
• A small number are in marine parks and aquariums, but there's a growing movement against keeping them in captivity due to their intelligence and need for large territories.

Countries/Areas of Natural Habitat:
• Found in all the world's oceans, from the polar regions to the equator, but commonly seen in areas like the Pacific Northwest, Norway, and Antarctica.

Interesting Facts:
1. Top of the Food Chain: Orcas are apex predators, meaning they are at the top of the food chain and have no natural predators.
2. Smart and Social: They live in complex social groups called pods, have their own languages, and can teach each other hunting techniques.
3. Diverse Diet: Different orca populations specialize in different types of food, including fish, seals, and even other whales.

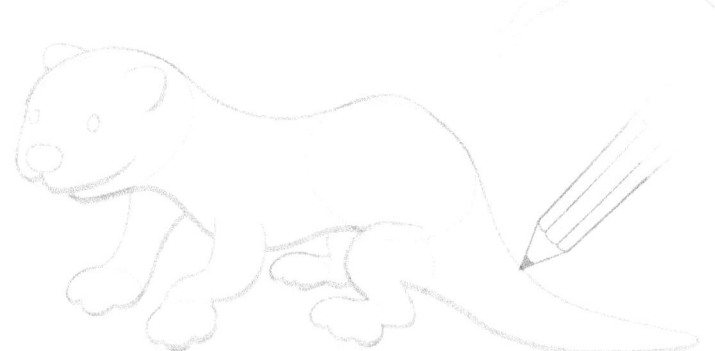

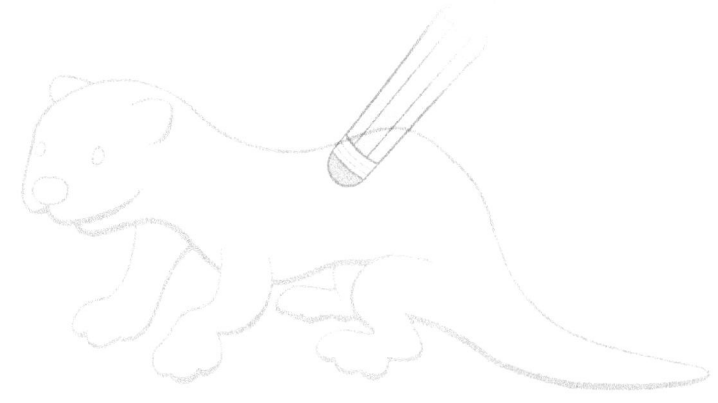

STEP 3: Erase the circles

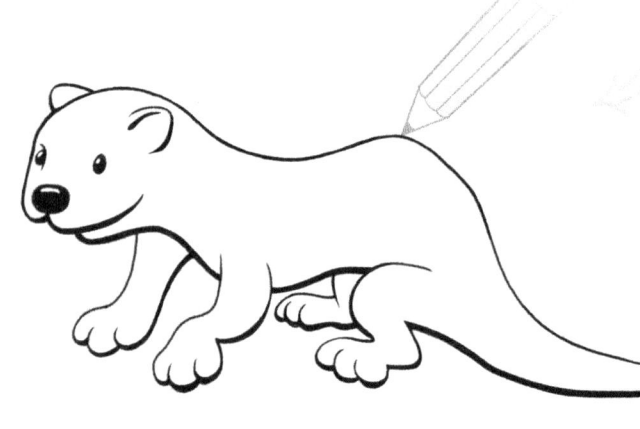

STEP 4 – FINISH:
Add details, Draw dark

DRAWING TIPS:

Try drawing some lines thick,
and other lines thin.

Try drawing different shaped eyes

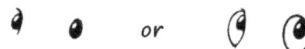 or

California Sea Otter

Use this as a guide for each of the steps in creating your own drawing.

Fun Facts:

California Sea Otter

Reasons for Endangerment:
1. Oil Spills: Oil from spills in the ocean can cover their fur, making it hard for them to stay warm and float.
2. Fishing Nets: Sometimes they get caught in fishing nets and can't get out, which can be very dangerous for them.
3. Pollution: Chemicals and trash in the water can make them sick or hurt the food they eat.

Population in the Wild:
- Around 3,000, mostly living along the central coast of California, but their numbers fluctuate due to various threats.

Population in Captivity:
- A small number are in aquariums and marine sanctuaries for conservation and education purposes.

Countries/Areas of Natural Habitat:
- Mainly found along the central coast of California, USA, in kelp forests and coastal areas.

Interesting Facts:
1. Tool Users: They are one of the few animal species that use tools. They use rocks to break open shellfish to eat.
2. Floating Naps: They often sleep in the water, floating on their backs. They sometimes hold hands in groups (called rafts) to stay together while they sleep.
3. Thick Fur: They have the densest fur of any animal, which keeps them warm in cold water but also requires constant grooming to stay clean and fluffy.

STEP 1 – START:
Draw light circles

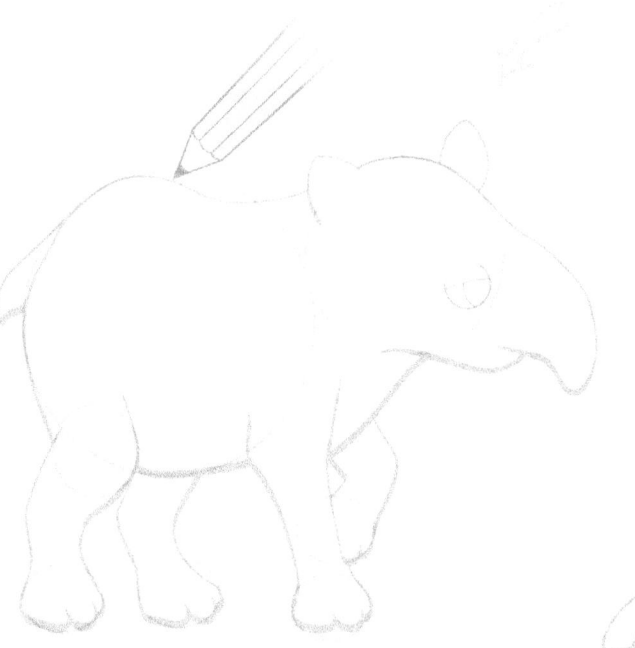

STEP 2: Draw light lines

STEP 3: Erase the circles

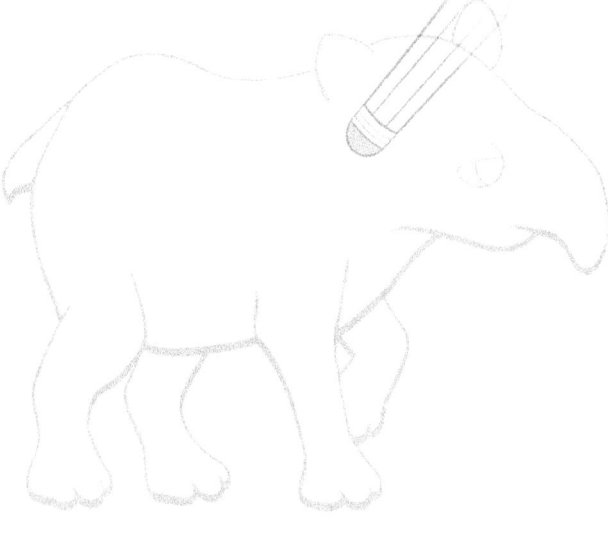

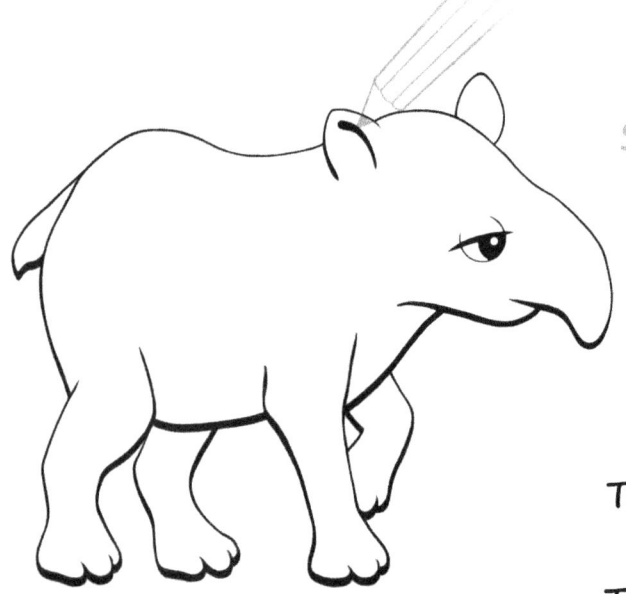

STEP 4 – FINISH:
Add details, Draw dark

DRAWING TIPS:

Try drawing some lines thick,
and other lines thin.

Try drawing different shaped eyes

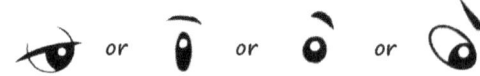

Central American Tapir

Use this as a guide for each of the steps in creating your own drawing.

Fun Facts:

Central American Tapir

Reasons for Endangerment:
1. Habitat Loss: Their home in the rainforest is being cut down for farming and to build houses, leaving them with less space to live and find food.
2. Hunting: Some people hunt them for food or sport, even though it's not allowed.
3. Roads and Development: Building roads and other structures in their habitat can divide their living space and make it hard for them to find mates or escape from predators.

Population in the Wild:
• Numbers are decreasing, but exact population is not well known due to their secretive nature and dense forest habitat.

Population in Captivity:
• They are kept in some zoos and wildlife sanctuaries where they are part of breeding and conservation programs.

Countries/Areas of Natural Habitat:
• Found in rainforests and swamps in Central America, including parts of Mexico, Belize, Guatemala, Honduras, Nicaragua, Costa Rica, and Panama.

Interesting Facts:
1. Unique Snout: They have a long, flexible snout that works a bit like an elephant's trunk. They use it to grab leaves and fruits to eat.
2. Swimming Skills: They are excellent swimmers and can use water as a place to hide from predators or cool off.
3. Nighttime Foragers: They are mostly active at night (nocturnal) and spend their nights searching for food like leaves, fruits, and twigs.

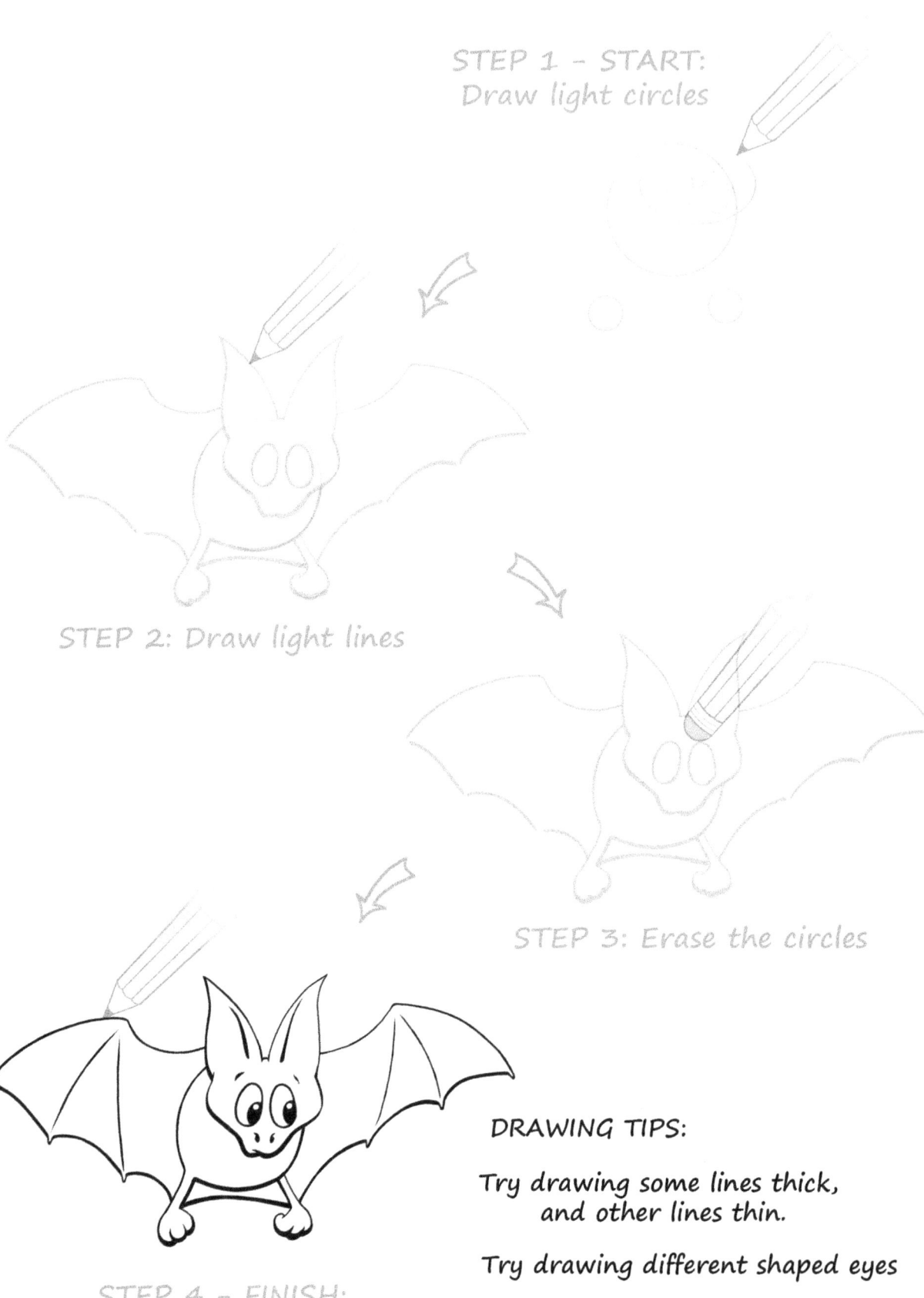

STEP 1 – START:
Draw light circles

STEP 2: Draw light lines

STEP 3: Erase the circles

STEP 4 – FINISH:
Add details, Draw dark

DRAWING TIPS:

Try drawing some lines thick,
and other lines thin.

Try drawing different shaped eyes

or

Sardinian Long-Eared Bat

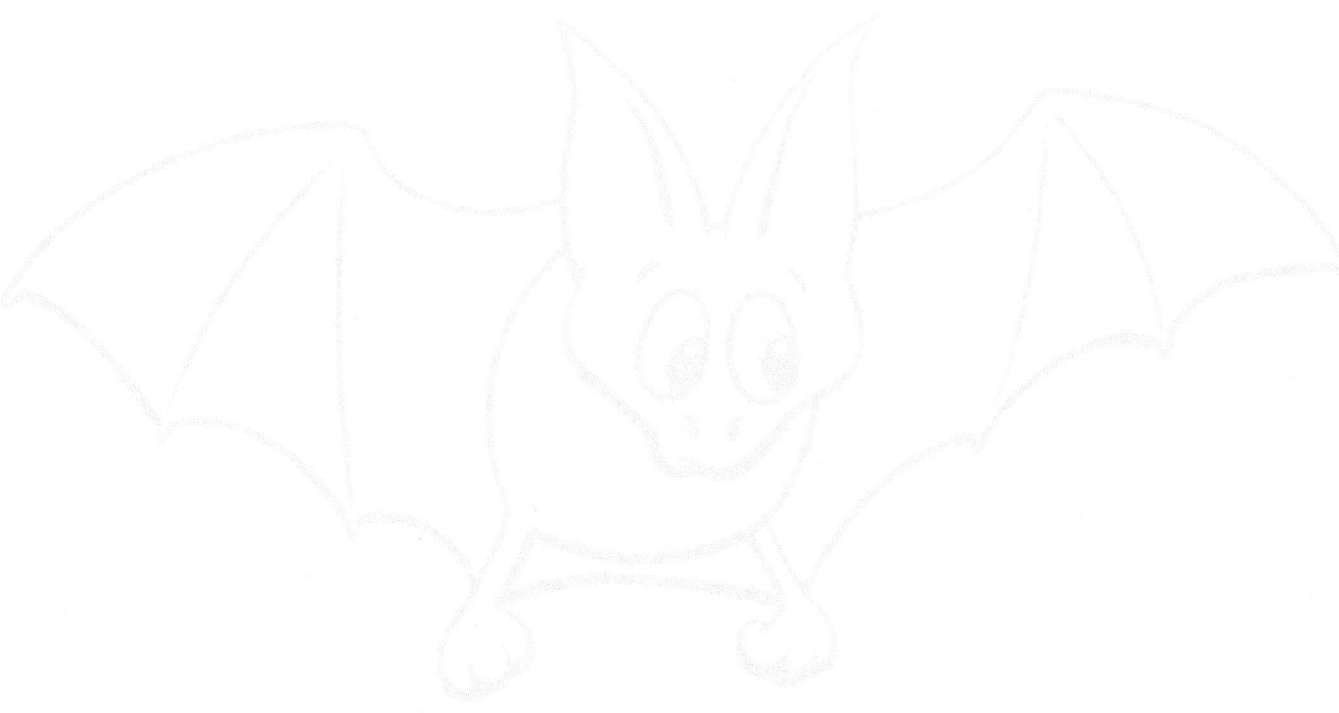

Use this as a guide
for each of the
steps in creating
your own drawing.

Fun Facts:

Sardinian Long-Eared Bat

Reasons for Endangerment:
   1. Habitat Disturbance: Their roosting places, like caves and old buildings, are being disturbed or destroyed
      by human activities.
   2. Pesticides: Chemicals used in farming can kill the insects they eat, leaving them with less food.
   3. Climate Change: Changes in weather patterns can affect their habitat and the availability of their food
      sources.
Population in the Wild:
   • Very rare, with only a few known roosting sites, making them one of Europe's most endangered bat species.
Population in Captivity:
   • Not typically kept in captivity due to their specific habitat and dietary needs.
Countries/Areas of Natural Habitat:
   • Found mainly in Sardinia, an island in the Mediterranean Sea, part of Italy.
Interesting Facts:
   1. Special Ears: They have very long ears, which they use to listen for the sounds of insects moving in the dark.
   2. Nighttime Hunters: They use echolocation to navigate and find food in the dark, sending out sound waves
      that bounce back to them from objects.
   3. Insect Diet: Their diet consists mainly of moths and other small flying insects, which they catch while flying.

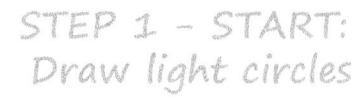

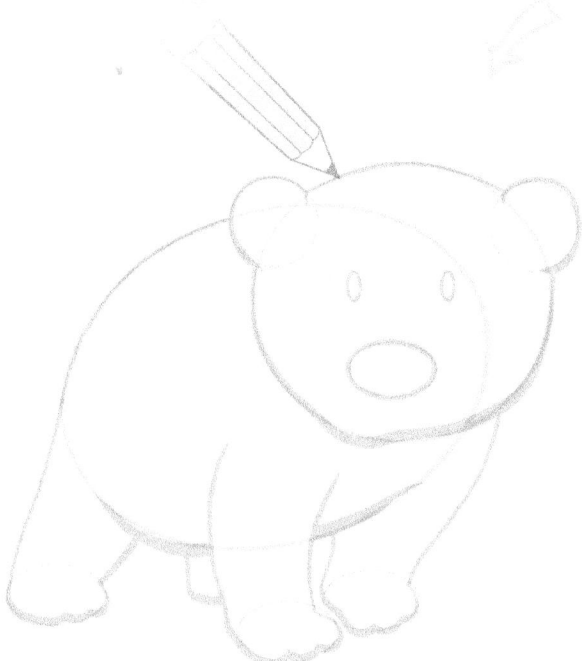

STEP 2: Draw light lines

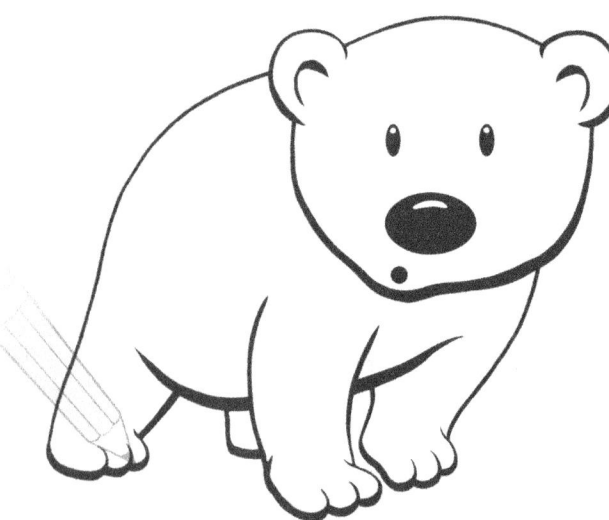

STEP 3: Erase the circles

STEP 4 - FINISH:
Add details, Draw dark

DRAWING TIPS:

Try drawing some lines thick,
and other lines thin.

Try drawing different shaped eyes

 or

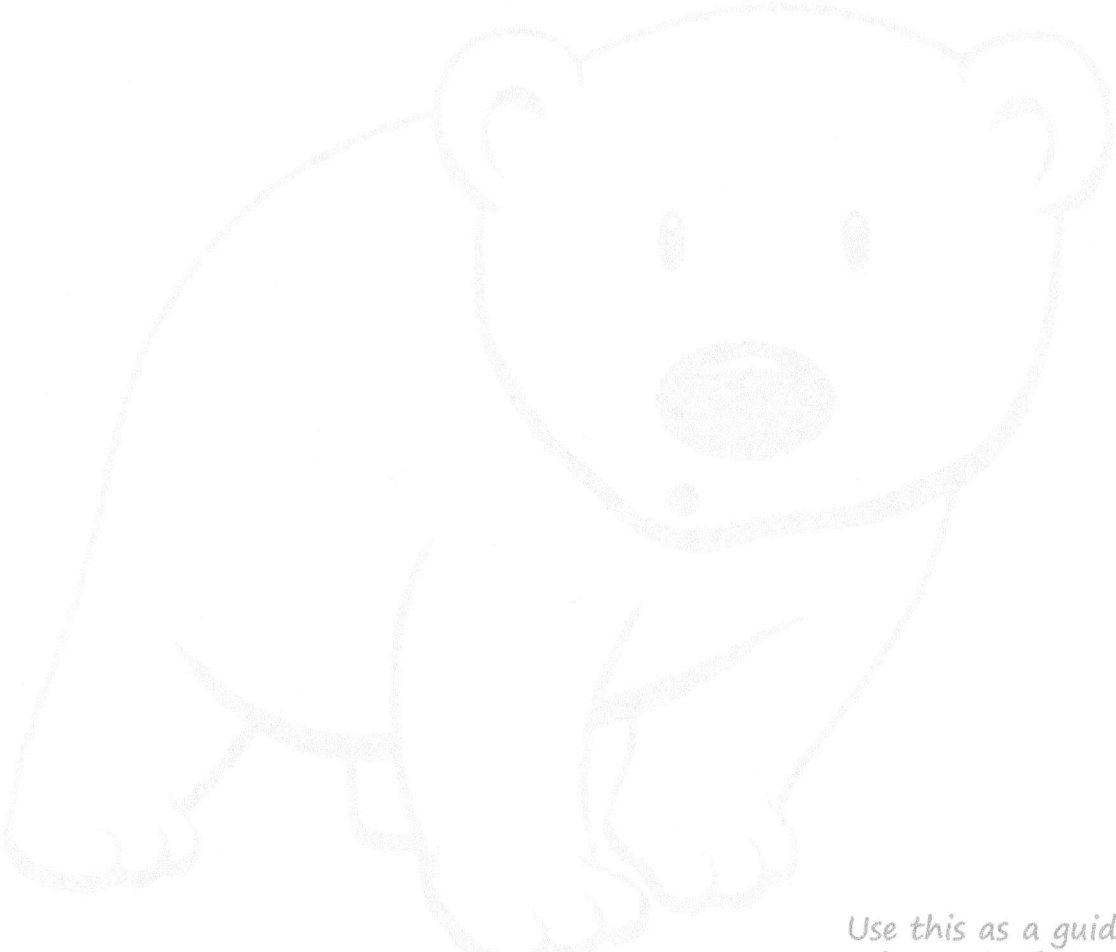

Polar Bear

Fun Facts:

Polar Bear

Reasons for Endangerment:
1. Climate Change: The ice in the Arctic, where they live, is melting, which makes it harder for them to find food and places to rest.
2. Pollution: Chemicals and waste in the ocean can make them sick and can also harm their food supply.
3. Oil and Gas Development: Drilling for oil and gas can disturb their habitat and can lead to oil spills, which are dangerous for them and their food.

Population in the Wild:
• Estimated to be around 22,000 to 31,000, but their numbers are threatened due to melting sea ice and other factors.

Population in Captivity:
• A number are in zoos around the world, where they are part of conservation and education programs.

Countries/Areas of Natural Habitat:
• Found in the Arctic region, across countries like Canada, Greenland, Norway, Russia, and the United States (Alaska).

Interesting Facts:
1. Marine Mammals: Although they live on ice, they are considered marine mammals because they depend so much on the ocean for food.
2. Powerful Swimmers: They can swim for long distances and can even swim for several hours to get from one piece of ice to another.
3. Insulated Fur: Their fur is not actually white; it's transparent and hollow, which helps trap the sun's heat to keep them warm. Their skin underneath is black to absorb as much heat as possible.

Use this as a guide for each of the steps in creating your own drawing.

STEP 1 – START:
Draw light circles

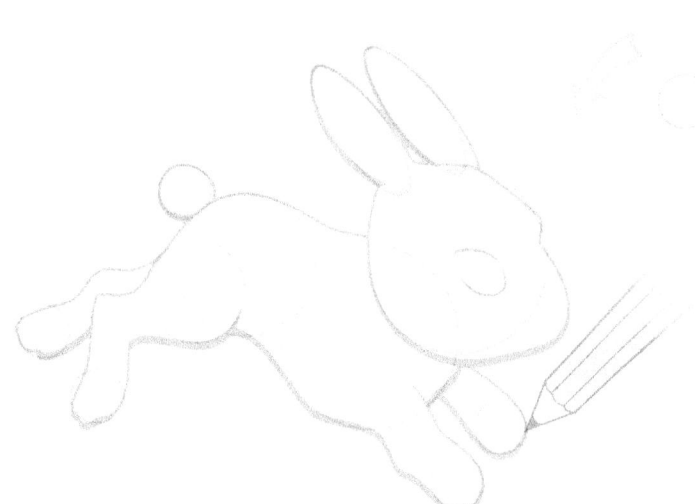

STEP 2: Draw light lines

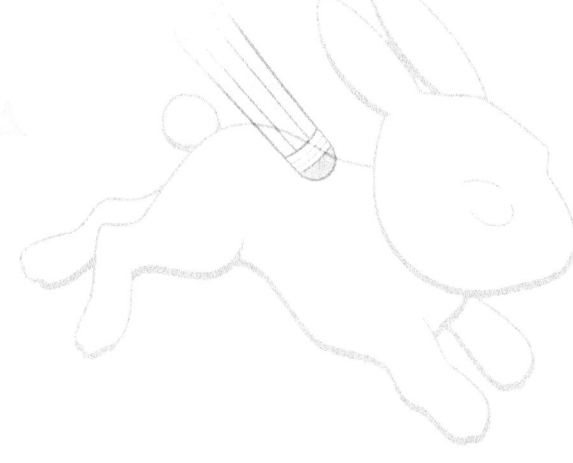

STEP 3: Erase the circles

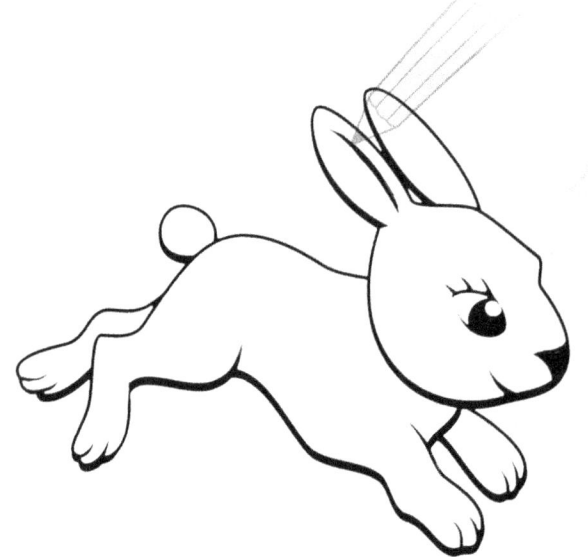

STEP 4 – FINISH:
Add details, Draw dark

DRAWING TIPS:

Try drawing some lines thick,
and other lines thin.

Try drawing different shaped eyes

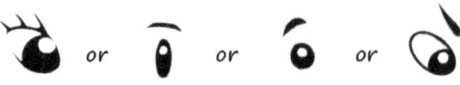

Riverine Rabbit

Use this as a guide
for each of the
steps in creating
your own drawing.

Fun Facts:

Riverine Rabbit

Reasons for Endangerment:
1. Habitat Loss: Their homes along riverbanks are being taken away for farming and building.
2. Overgrazing: Farm animals eating too much of the plants in the area can damage the habitat the rabbits need to live and hide from predators.
3. Human Disturbance: Building and farming activities can disturb their living areas and make it hard for them to find food and shelter.

Population in the Wild:
• Very few, estimated to be around 250 mature individuals, making them one of the most endangered mammals in the world.

Population in Captivity:
• Very rare in captivity due to their specific habitat needs and low reproductive rates.

Countries/Areas of Natural Habitat:
• Found only in certain parts of South Africa, especially in the Karoo region.

Interesting Facts:
1. Unique Nesting: They are the only African rabbit that builds a nest for its young.
2. Rare Sightings: They are nocturnal and very shy, making them one of the least seen and most elusive rabbits.
3. Conservation Efforts: There are special programs aimed at protecting their habitat and educating people about the importance of saving this unique species.

STEP 1 - START:
Draw light circles

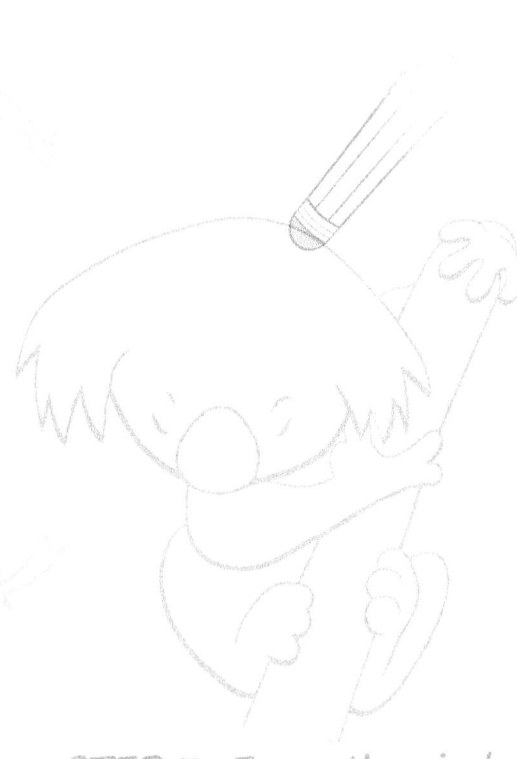

STEP 2: Draw light lines

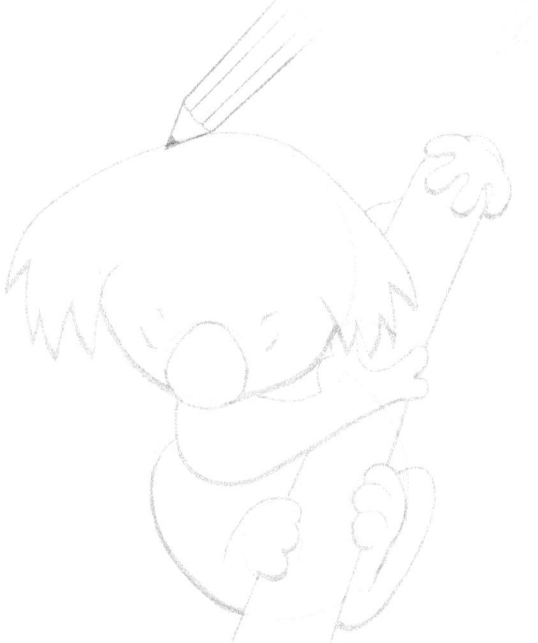

STEP 3: Erase the circles

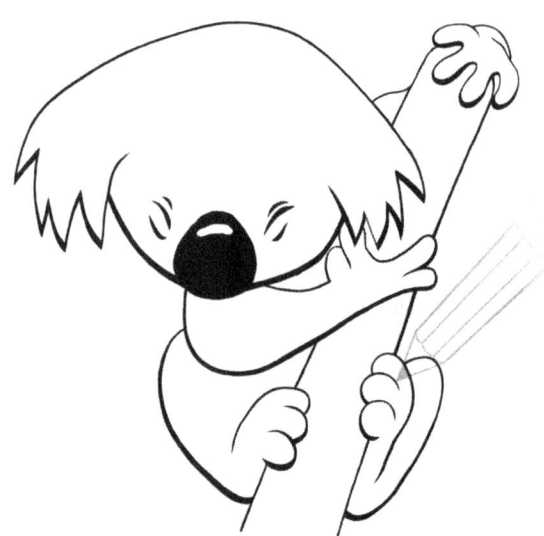

STEP 4 - FINISH:
Add details, Draw dark

DRAWING TIPS:

Try drawing some lines thick, and other lines thin.

Try drawing different shaped eyes

  or

Koala

Use this as a guide for each of the steps in creating your own drawing.

Fun Facts:

Koala

Reasons for Endangerment:
1. Habitat Loss: Their homes in eucalyptus forests are being cut down for cities, farms, and roads.
2. Disease: Many koalas get sick from a disease called chlamydia, which can hurt their eyes and make it hard for them to have babies.
3. Bushfires and Climate Change: Large bushfires can destroy their homes and food, and changes in climate can also affect the eucalyptus trees they depend on.

Population in the Wild:
• Estimated to be less than 100,000, but numbers are declining due to habitat loss and other threats.

Population in Captivity:
• Found in various zoos and wildlife sanctuaries, especially in Australia, where they are part of conservation and rehabilitation programs.

Countries/Areas of Natural Habitat:
• Found in the wild only in Australia, mainly in the eastern and southern regions where there are eucalyptus forests and woodlands.

Interesting Facts:
1. Picky Eaters: They eat mainly eucalyptus leaves and are very picky, eating leaves from only a few types of eucalyptus trees.
2. Sleepyheads: Koalas sleep up to 18-22 hours a day because their diet requires a lot of energy to digest and doesn't provide much energy.
3. Fingerprints: Their fingerprints are so similar to human fingerprints that they can sometimes be confused at a crime scene!

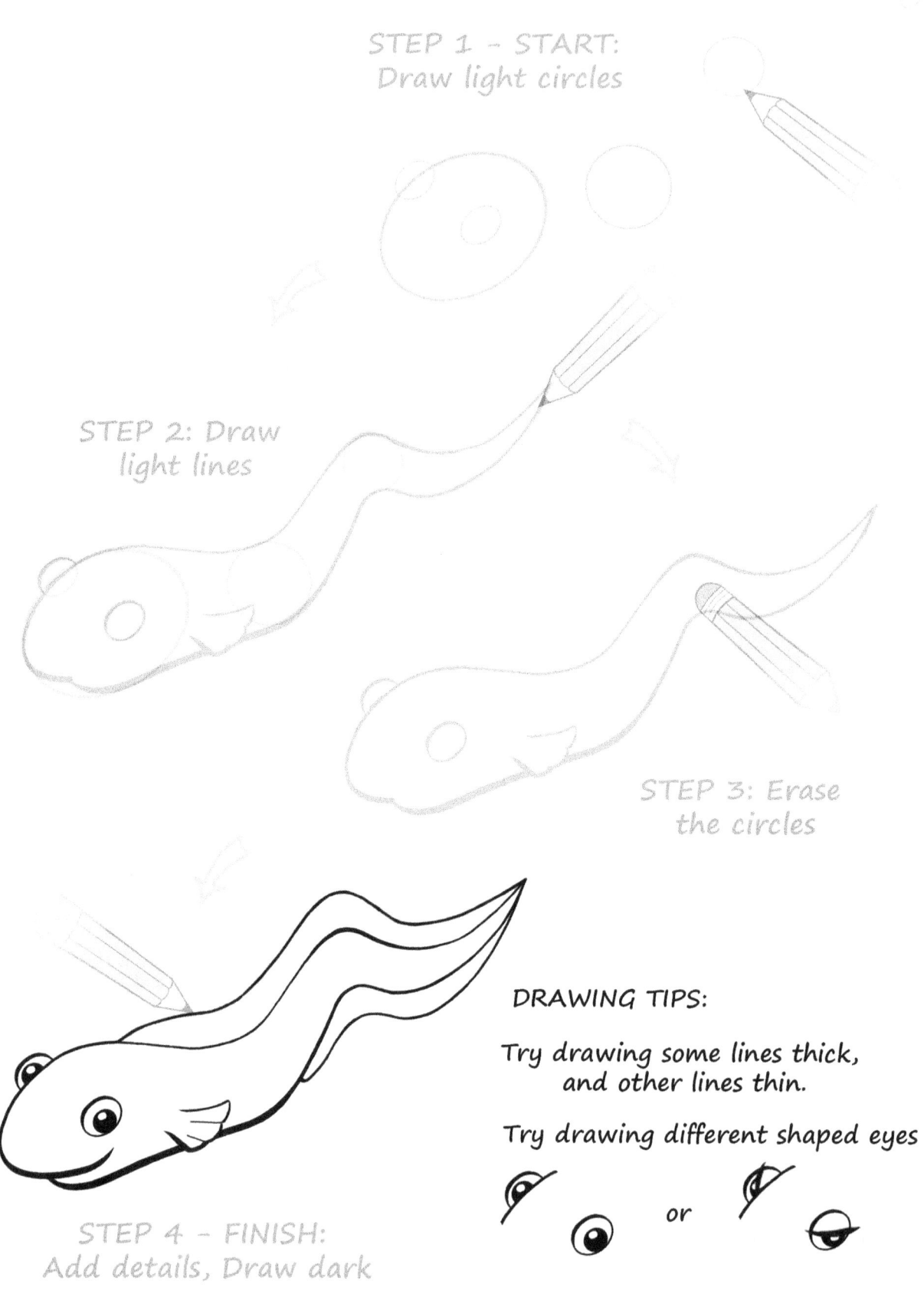

STEP 1 – START:
Draw light circles

STEP 2: Draw
light lines

STEP 3: Erase
the circles

STEP 4 – FINISH:
Add details, Draw dark

DRAWING TIPS:

Try drawing some lines thick,
and other lines thin.

Try drawing different shaped eyes

or

European Eel

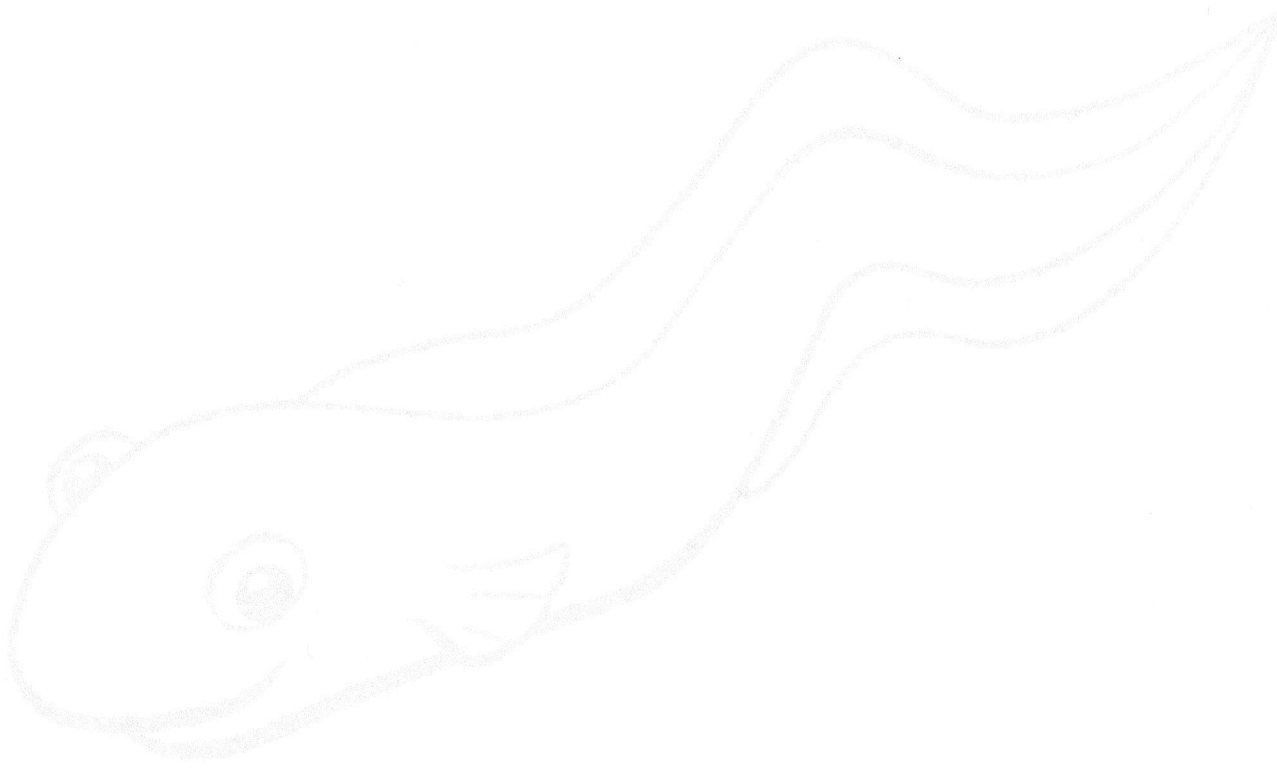

Fun Facts:

European Eel

Reasons for Endangerment:
1. Overfishing: They are caught in large numbers for food, which has greatly reduced their population.
2. Habitat Changes: Building dams and other structures in rivers can block their migration routes and make it hard for them to travel to their breeding grounds.
3. Pollution: Water pollution can harm the eels and the creatures they eat, making it hard for them to survive.

Population in the Wild:
• Their numbers have decreased by about 90% in the last few decades, making them critically endangered.

Population in Captivity:
• They are kept and bred in some aquaculture facilities for food, but breeding them successfully in captivity is challenging.

Countries/Areas of Natural Habitat:
• Found in rivers, lakes, and coastal areas across Europe and parts of North Africa.

Interesting Facts:
1. Mysterious Migration: They are born in the Sargasso Sea and then travel thousands of miles to freshwaters in Europe. After many years, they return to the Sargasso Sea to lay eggs and then die, completing their life cycle.
2. Slippery and Slimy: They have a slimy coating on their skin, which makes them slippery and helps protect them from diseases and parasites.
3. Can Breathe Through Skin: While they have gills, they can also absorb oxygen through their skin, which is helpful when they travel over land during wet nights to reach new waters.

Use this as a guide for each of the steps in creating your own drawing.

STEP 1 – START:
Draw light circles

STEP 2: Draw light lines

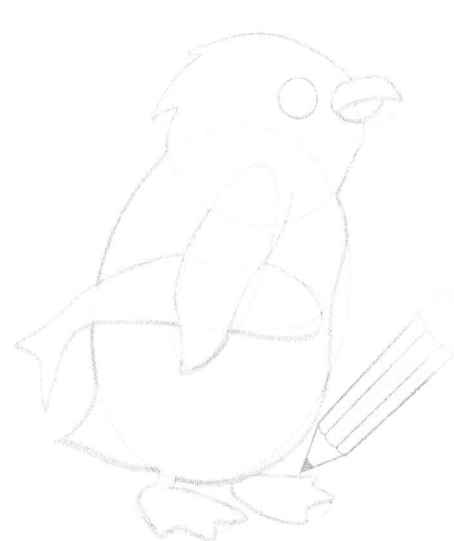

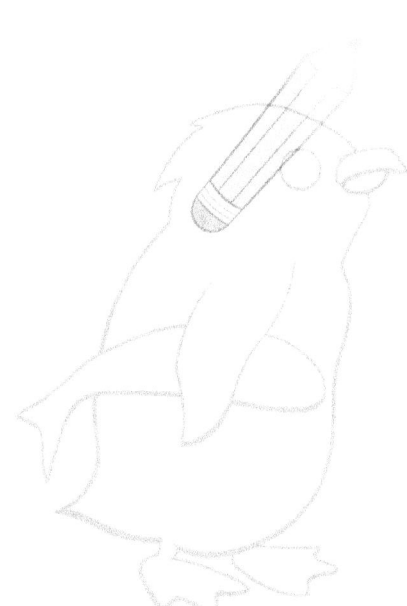

STEP 3: Erase the circles

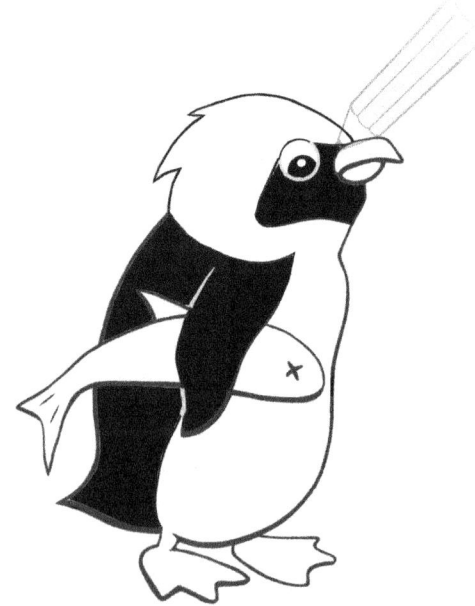

STEP 4 – FINISH:
Add details, Draw dark

DRAWING TIPS:

Try drawing some lines thick,
and other lines thin.

Try drawing different shaped eyes

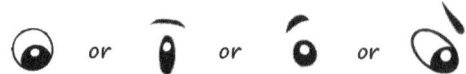 or   or   or

African Penguin

Use this as a guide
for each of the
steps in creating
your own drawing.

Fun Facts:

African Penguin

Reasons for Endangerment:
1. Oil Spills: Oil from ships can pollute the water and beaches where they live, making it hard for them to stay clean and find food.
2. Overfishing: When there's less fish in the sea, it's harder for them to find enough to eat.
3. Habitat Disturbance: Their nesting areas can be disturbed by human activities, like tourism and development.

Population in the Wild:
• Around 50,000, but their numbers have been decreasing over the years.

Population in Captivity:
• Some are kept in zoos and aquariums where they are part of breeding and conservation programs.

Countries/Areas of Natural Habitat:
• Found along the southern coast of Africa, especially in South Africa and Namibia.

Interesting Facts:
1. Braying Call: They are also known as "jackass penguins" because of their loud, donkey-like call.
2. Tuxedo Look: They have a distinctive black and white coloring, which helps camouflage them in the water from predators.
3. Swimming Speedsters: They are excellent swimmers, using their wings to 'fly' through the water, and can reach speeds up to 12 miles per hour.

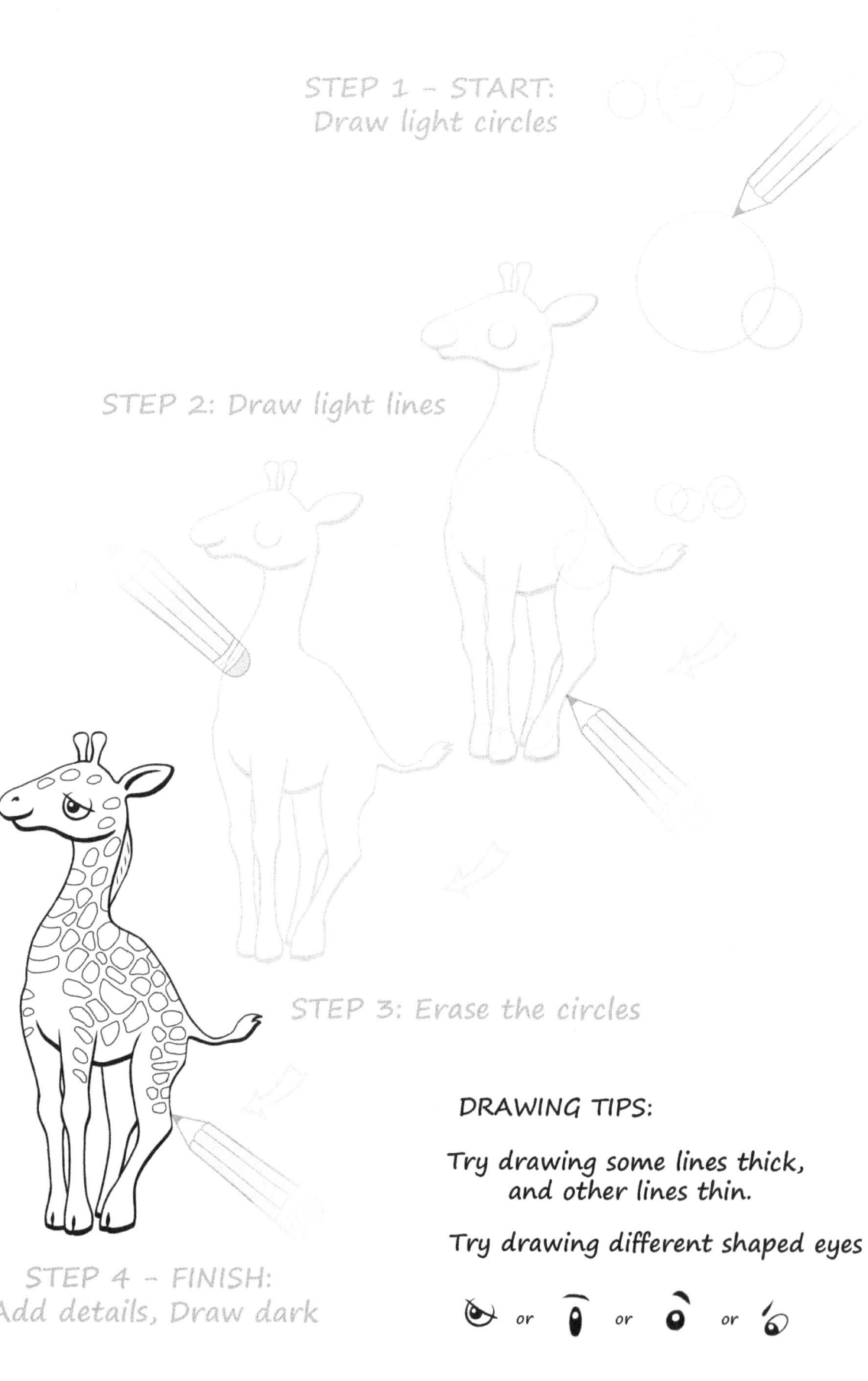

STEP 1 - START:
Draw light circles

STEP 2: Draw light lines

STEP 3: Erase the circles

STEP 4 - FINISH:
Add details, Draw dark

DRAWING TIPS:

Try drawing some lines thick,
and other lines thin.

Try drawing different shaped eyes

or   or   or

Nubian Giraffe

Use this as a guide
for each of the
steps in creating
your own drawing.

Fun Facts:

Nubian Giraffe

Reasons for Endangerment:
1. Habitat Loss: Their living spaces are being taken over for farming or building, leaving them with fewer places to live and find food.
2. Poaching: Some people illegally hunt them for their skin and meat.
3. Civil Unrest: Conflicts and wars in some of the areas where they live can make it hard for them to survive and for conservationists to protect them.

Population in the Wild:
• Very few, with estimates around a few thousand, making them one of the more endangered types of giraffes.

Population in Captivity:
• Some are kept in zoos around the world as part of breeding and conservation programs.

Countries/Areas of Natural Habitat:
• Found in parts of East Africa, including Ethiopia, South Sudan, and Uganda.

Interesting Facts:
1. Tallest Animals: Giraffes are the tallest land animals. The Nubian giraffe can reach up to 18 feet tall!
2. Unique Patterns: They have a unique pattern of spots that are larger and more irregular than other types of giraffes, and no two giraffes have the same pattern.
3. Long Tongue: They have a long, prehensile tongue (about 18 inches) that they use to grab leaves and branches from trees.

STEP 1 – START:
Draw light circles

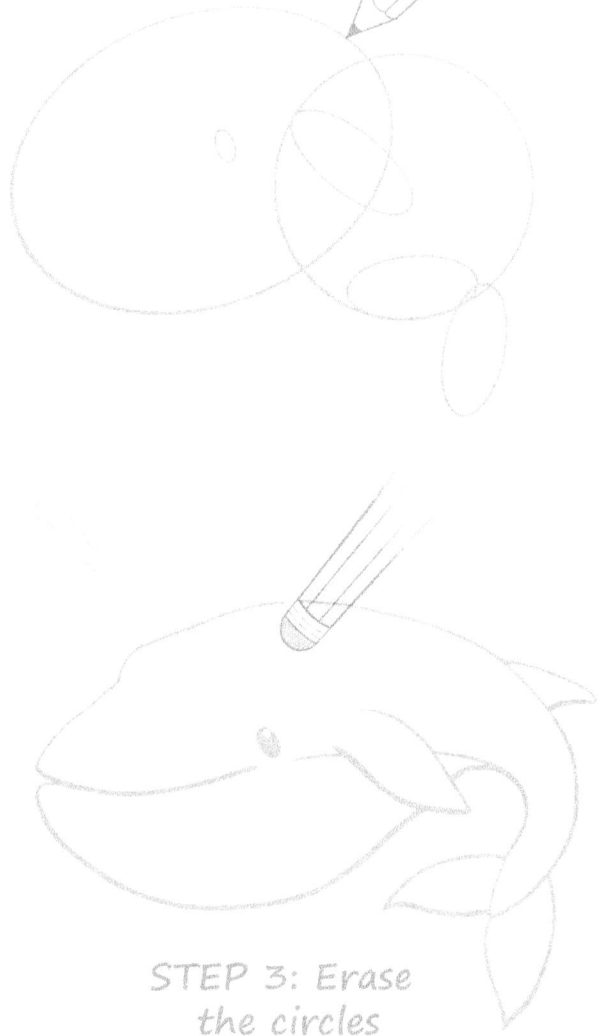

STEP 2: Draw
light lines

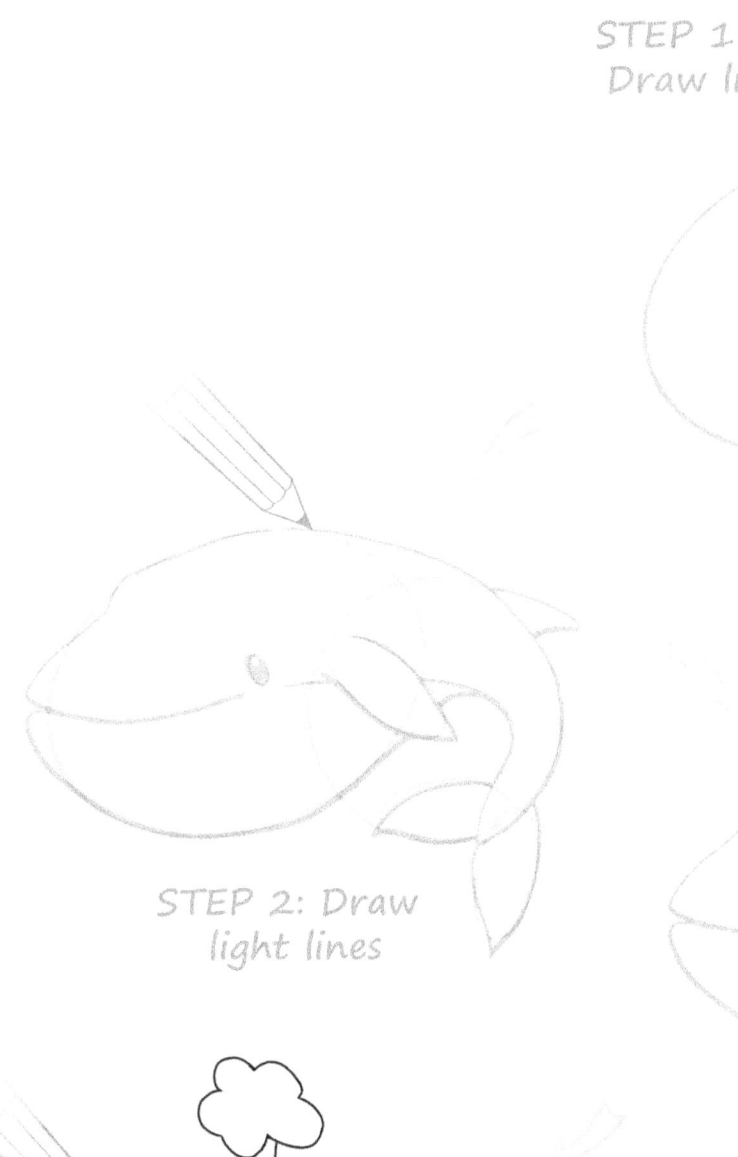

STEP 3: Erase
the circles

STEP 4 – FINISH:
Add details, Draw dark

DRAWING TIPS:

Try drawing some lines thick,
and other lines thin.

Try drawing different shaped eyes

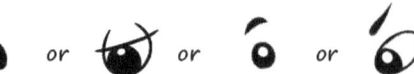

Blue Whale

Use this as a guide
for each of the
steps in creating
your own drawing.

Fun Facts:

Blue Whale

Reasons for Endangerment:
1. Whaling: In the past, they were hunted a lot for their oil and body parts, which greatly reduced their numbers.
2. Ship Strikes: Sometimes they can get hit by large ships, which can be very dangerous for them.
3. Ocean Pollution: The water they live in can get polluted with chemicals and plastics, which can harm their health and food supply.

Population in the Wild:
• Estimated to be between 10,000 and 25,000, but they are slowly recovering from past hunting.

Population in Captivity:
• None, as they are far too large and need the open ocean to survive.

Countries/Areas of Natural Habitat:
• Found in all the world's oceans, from the Arctic to the Antarctic.

Interesting Facts:
1. Largest Animal Ever: They are the largest animal to have ever lived on Earth, even bigger than the biggest dinosaurs.
2. Loud Calls: Their calls can be louder than a jet engine and can be heard for many miles underwater.
3. Big Eaters: They eat a lot of tiny creatures called krill, and during feeding season, they can eat up to 4 tons of krill a day!

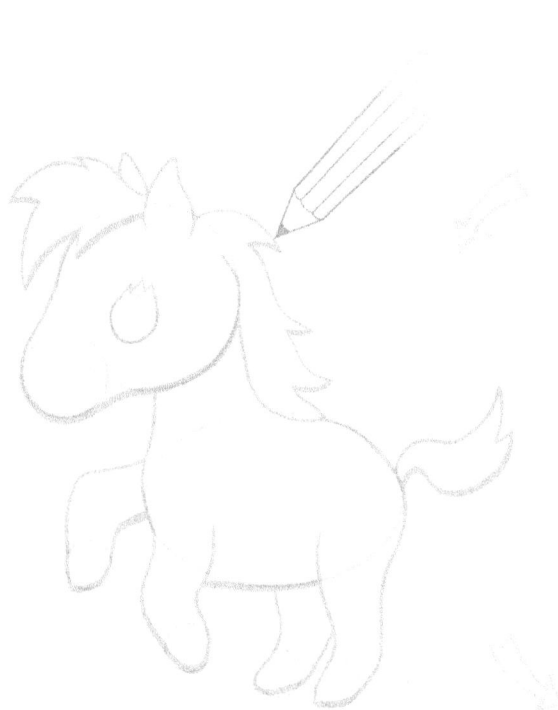

STEP 2: Draw light lines

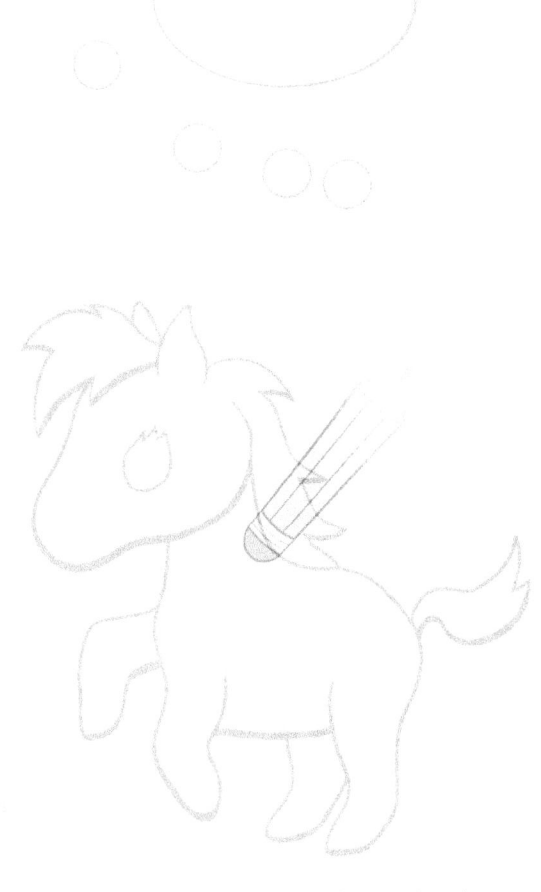

STEP 3: Erase the circles

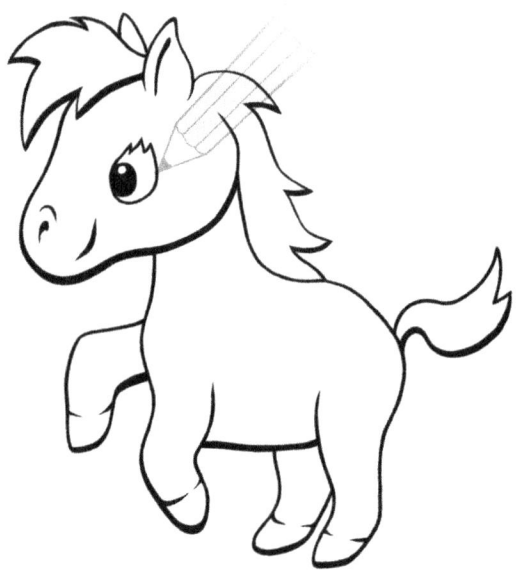

STEP 4 – FINISH:
Add details, Draw dark

DRAWING TIPS:

Try drawing some lines thick,
and other lines thin.

Try drawing different shaped eyes

 or or or

Przewalski's Wild Horse

Use this as a guide
for each of the
steps in creating
your own drawing.

Fun Facts:

Przewalski's Wild Horse

Reasons for Endangerment:
1. Habitat Loss: Their grazing land is being taken over for farming and other human activities.
2. Competition for Water and Food: They have to compete with livestock (like sheep and cattle) for water and grass, which can be tough.
3. Past Hunting: They were hunted in the past, which greatly reduced their numbers.

Population in the Wild:
- Around 2,000, thanks to successful reintroduction programs. However, they are still considered rare and vulnerable.

Population in Captivity:
- Around 1,500 in zoos and breeding centers around the world, where they are part of important conservation efforts.

Countries/Areas of Natural Habitat:
- They used to roam across much of Central Asia. Now, they are mostly found in Mongolia, specifically in areas like Hustai National Park and the Gobi Desert.

Interesting Facts:
1. Truly Wild: Przewalski's horse is the only true wild horse species left in the world. All other "wild" horses, like mustangs, are feral horses from domesticated stock.
2. Tough Survivors: They are well-adapted to living in harsh environments like the steppes and semi-desert areas of Mongolia.
3. Unique Look: They have a stocky build, a pale belly, and a dark, upright mane, which makes them look quite different from domesticated horses.

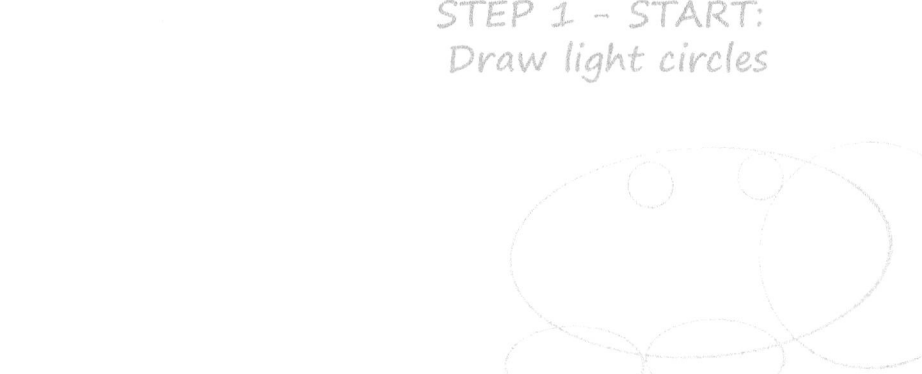

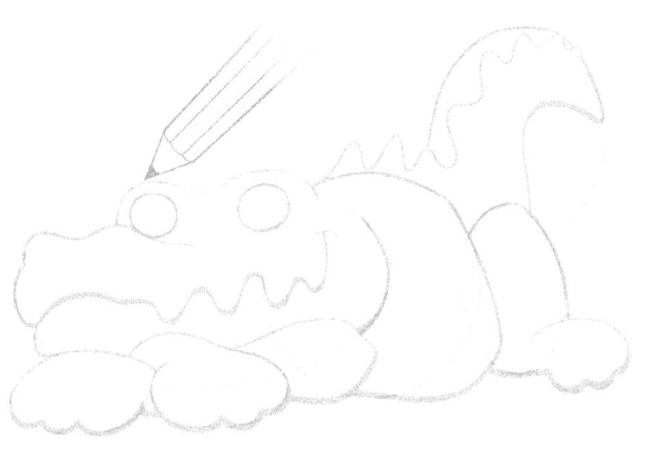

STEP 2: Draw light lines

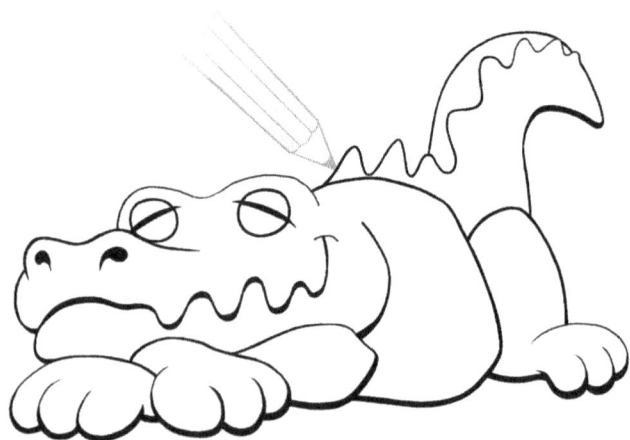

STEP 3: Erase the circles

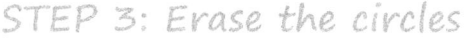

STEP 4 – FINISH:
Add details, Draw dark

DRAWING TIPS:

Try drawing some lines thick,
and other lines thin.

Try drawing different shaped eyes

  or

Philippine Crocodile

Use this as a guide
for each of the
steps in creating
your own drawing.

Fun Facts:

Philippine Crocodile

Reasons for Endangerment:
  1. Hunting: They were hunted a lot in the past for their skin and meat.
  2. Habitat Loss: Their homes in freshwater areas are being changed for farming and other human activities.
  3. Negative Image: Sometimes they are killed because people are afraid of them or think they are pests.
Population in the Wild:
  • Very few, estimated to be around 100-200 adults, making them one of the most critically endangered
    crocodile species.
Population in Captivity:
  • Found in some conservation centers and zoos, where breeding programs are helping to increase their numbers.
Countries/Areas of Natural Habitat:
  • Found only in the Philippines, mainly in freshwater habitats like rivers, ponds, and marshes.
Interesting Facts:
  1. Smaller Size: They are relatively small compared to other crocodile species, usually growing only up to 10
    feet long.
  2. Shy Nature: They are generally shy and avoid humans, preferring to live in quiet, remote areas.
  3. Protective Parents: The female Philippine crocodiles are very protective of their nests and young, guarding
    them fiercely against predators.

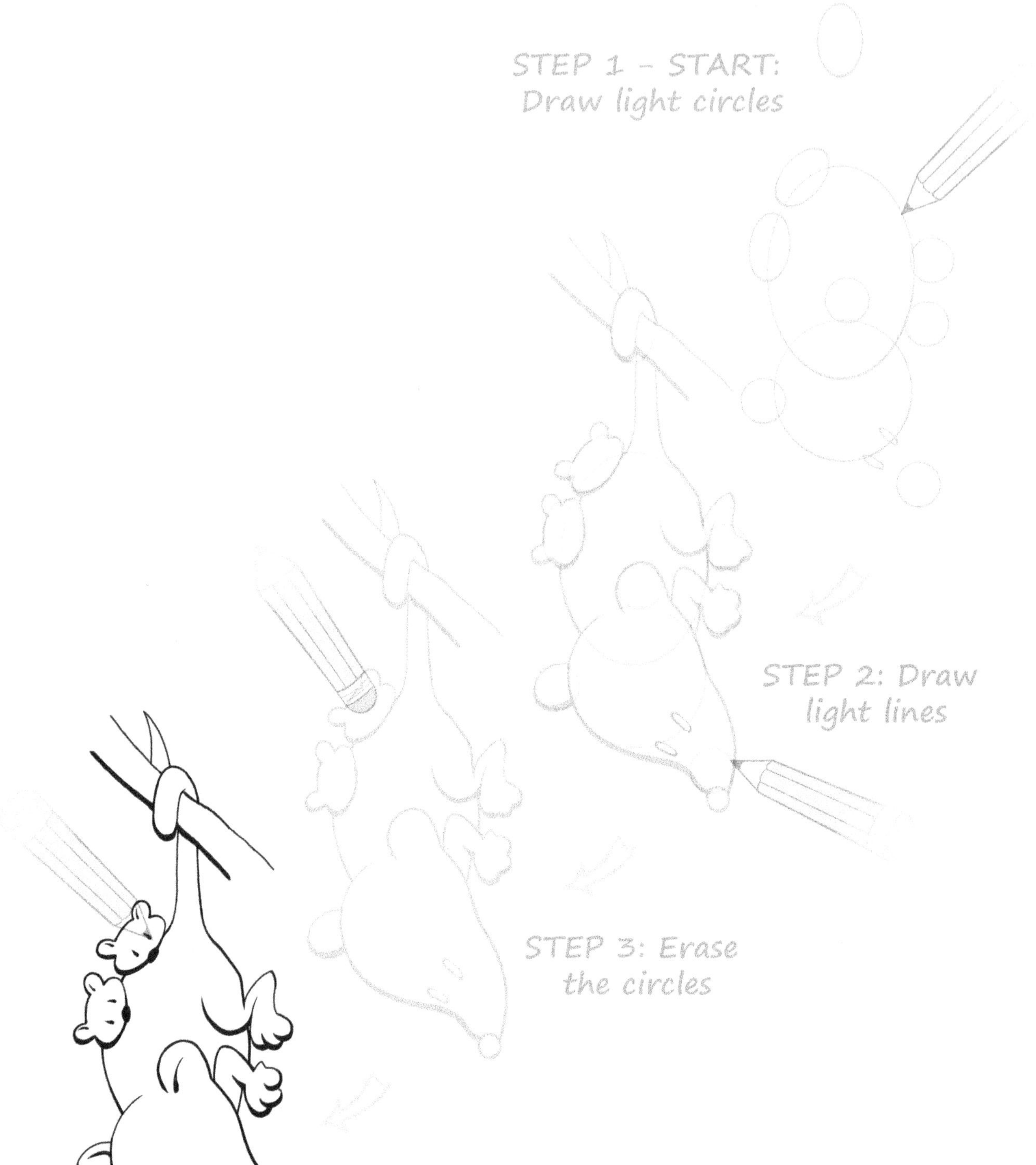

STEP 1 – START:
Draw light circles

STEP 2: Draw
light lines

STEP 3: Erase
the circles

STEP 4 – FINISH:
Add details, Draw dark

DRAWING TIPS:

Try drawing some lines thick,
and other lines thin.

Try drawing different shaped eyes

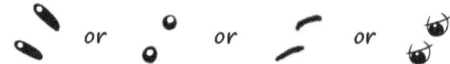

Mountain Pygmy Opossum

Use this as a guide
for each of the
steps in creating
your own drawing.

Fun Facts:

Mountain Pygmy Opossum

Reasons for Endangerment:
1. Habitat Loss: Their home in the mountain areas is being affected by ski resort development and other human activities.
2. Climate Change: Changes in climate can reduce the snow cover they rely on for insulation and affect their food sources.
3. Predation and Road Mortality: They are sometimes preyed upon by introduced species, and roads can be dangerous for them when they cross in search of food or mates.

Population in the Wild:
• Estimated to be less than 2,000 individuals, making them very rare and vulnerable.

Population in Captivity:
• Very few, mainly in specialized breeding and conservation programs.

Countries/Areas of Natural Habitat:
• Found only in the alpine and sub-alpine regions of the Australian states of Victoria and New South Wales.

Interesting Facts:
1. Winter Sleepers: They hibernate during the winter, curling up in a tight ball in rock crevices or under snow.
2. Tiny Climbers: Despite their small size, they are good climbers and can navigate through the rocky terrain of their mountain habitat.
3. Unique Diet: Their diet is mainly made up of insects and other small invertebrates, but during the spring, they also feed on the nectar of mountain plum-pine, a mutualistic relationship where they also help pollinate the plant.

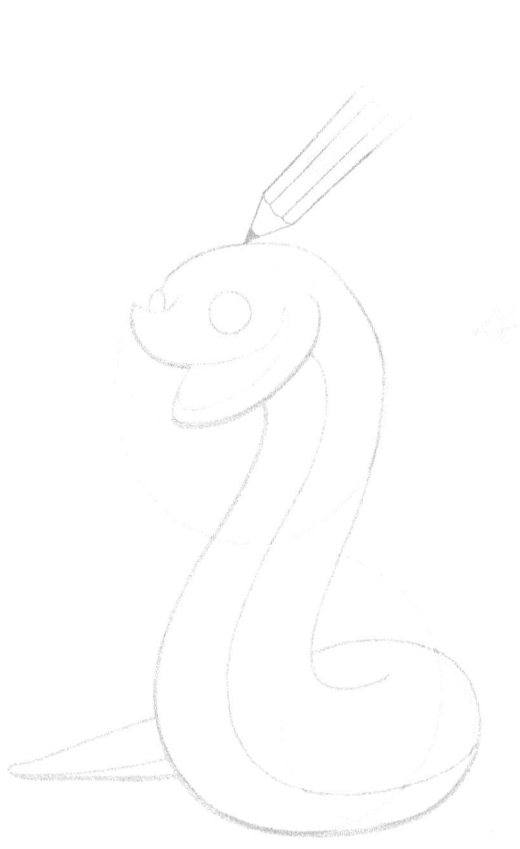

STEP 2: Draw light lines

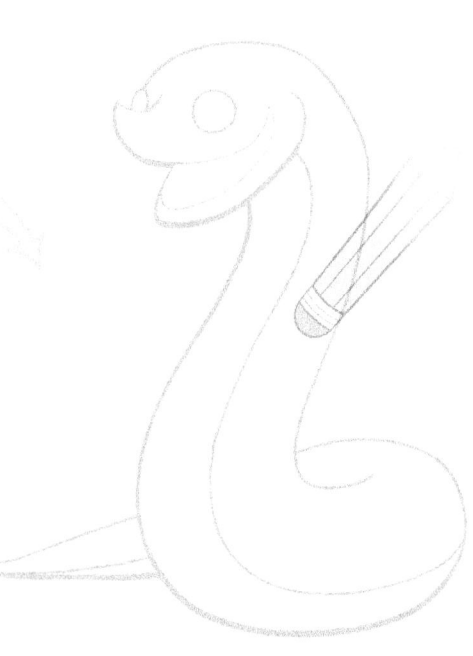

STEP 3: Erase the circles

DRAWING TIPS:

Try drawing some lines thick,
and other lines thin.

Try drawing different shaped eyes

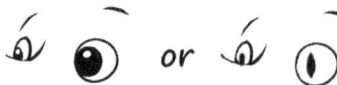

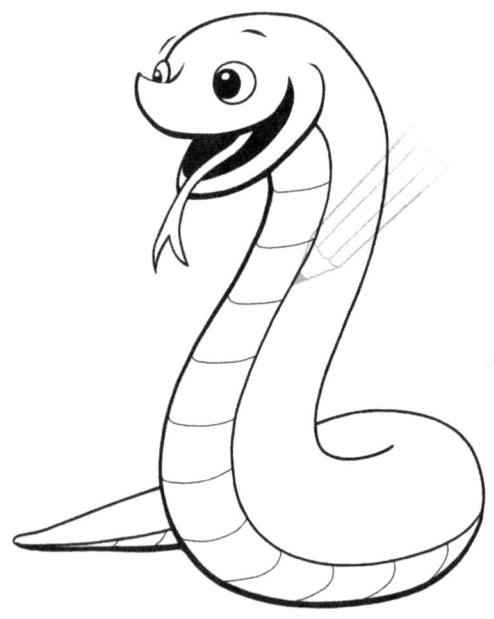

STEP 4 – FINISH:
Add details, Draw dark

Southern Hog-Nosed Snake

Use this as a guide
for each of the
steps in creating
your own drawing.

Fun Facts:

Southern Hog-nosed Snake

Reasons for Endangerment:
   1. Habitat Loss: Their homes in sandy forests and grasslands are being changed into places for people to live
      and for farming.
   2. Pesticides: Chemicals used in farming can kill the insects and small animals they eat.
   3. Road Mortality: Many are hit by cars when they try to cross roads that go through their natural habitats.
Population in the Wild:
   • Not well-known, but their numbers are believed to be decreasing and they are considered a species of concern.
Population in Captivity:
   • Sometimes kept by reptile enthusiasts, but they are not very common in captivity.
Countries/Areas of Natural Habitat:
   • Found in the southeastern United States, especially in states like Florida, Georgia, and South Carolina.
Interesting Facts:
   1. Distinctive Nose: They have an upturned snout, which they use to dig in the sand and soil to find food and
      make burrows.
   2. Playing Dead: When threatened, they might play dead by flipping onto their back and opening their mouth,
      sometimes even sticking out their tongue.
   3. Diet: Their diet mainly consists of toads, but they also eat other small amphibians and insects.

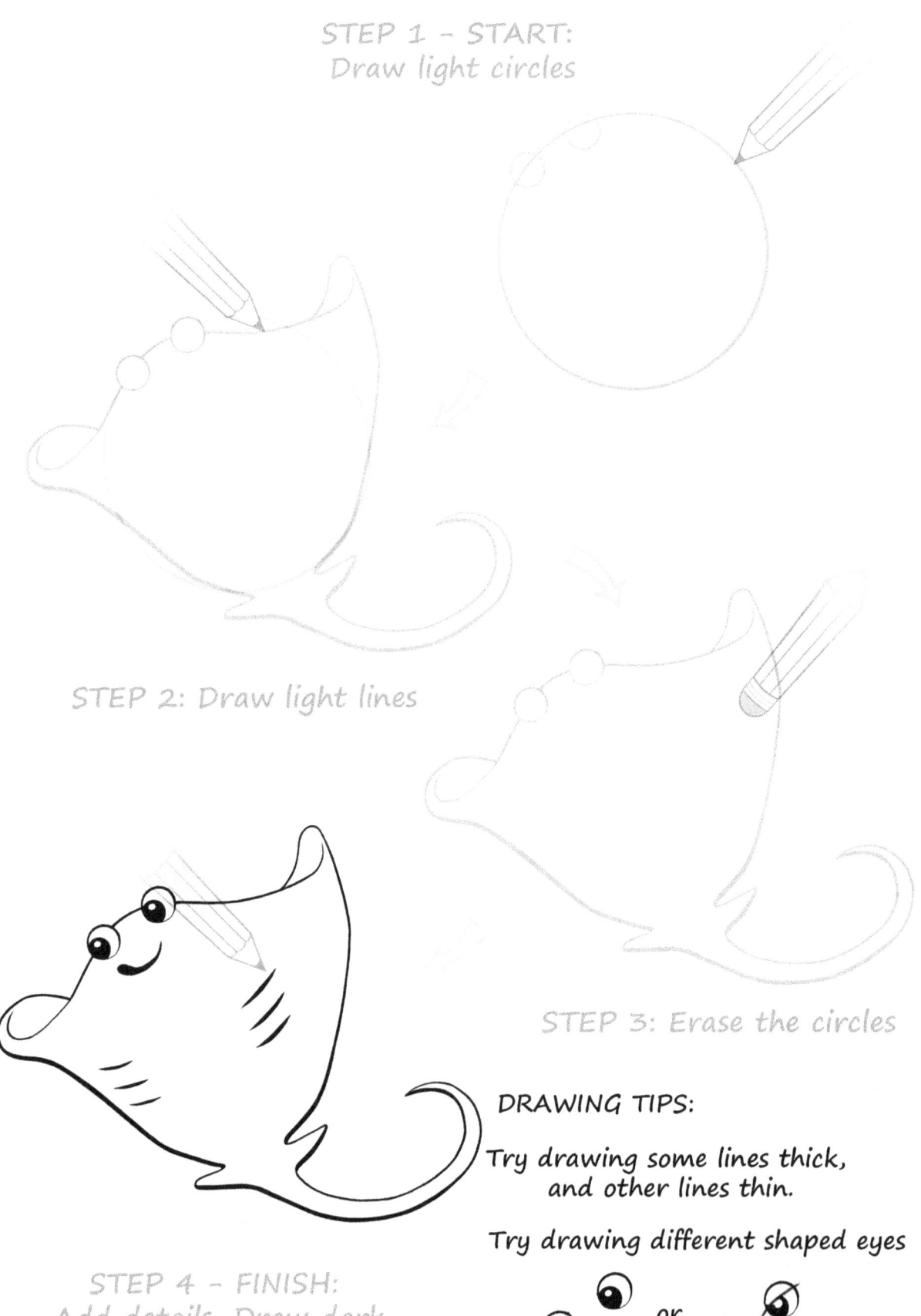

STEP 1 – START:
Draw light circles

STEP 2: Draw light lines

STEP 3: Erase the circles

DRAWING TIPS:

Try drawing some lines thick,
and other lines thin.

Try drawing different shaped eyes

or

STEP 4 – FINISH:
Add details, Draw dark

Giant Freshwater Stingray

Use this as a guide
for each of the
steps in creating
your own drawing.

Fun Facts:

Giant Freshwater Stingray

Reasons for Endangerment:
1. Overfishing: They are often caught by accident in fishing nets or intentionally for their meat.
2. Habitat Destruction: The rivers and lakes where they live are being polluted or changed by building dams and other structures.
3. Pollution: Water pollution from cities and farms can make their home dirty and unhealthy.

Population in the Wild:
• Not precisely known, but their numbers are believed to be decreasing due to the threats they face.

Population in Captivity:
• Very rare in captivity due to their large size and specific habitat needs.

Countries/Areas of Natural Habitat:
• Found in large rivers and lakes in Southeast Asia, including Thailand, Cambodia, Indonesia, and Malaysia.

Interesting Facts:
1. Huge Size: They are one of the largest freshwater fish in the world. Some can be as big as a car!
2. Mysterious Creatures: They spend a lot of time hidden in the mud at the bottom of rivers, which makes them hard to study and understand.
3. Electric Sensors: They have special sensors that help them find food in the muddy water where they can't see very well.

STEP 1 – START:
Draw light circles

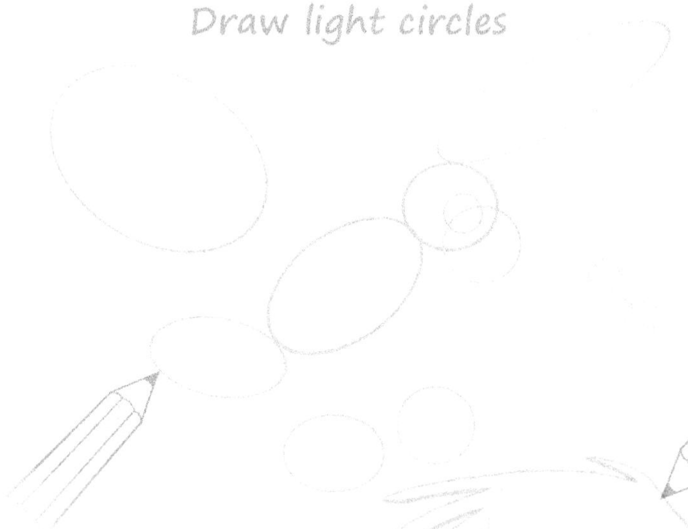

STEP 2: Draw light lines

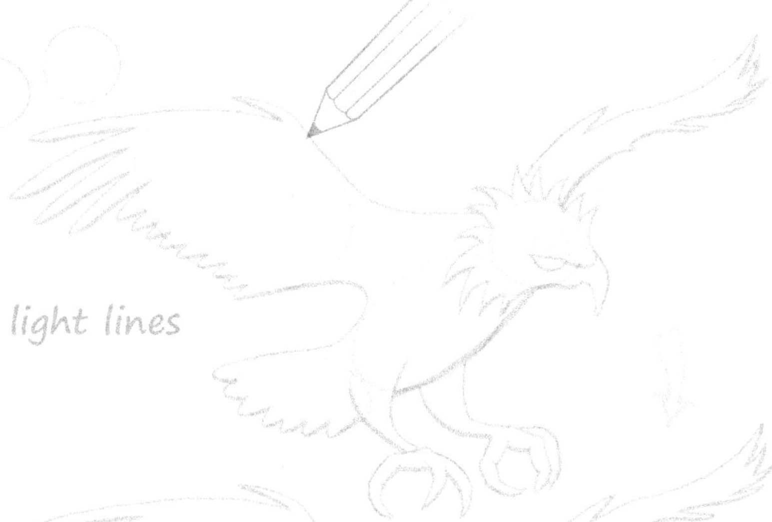

STEP 3: Erase the circles

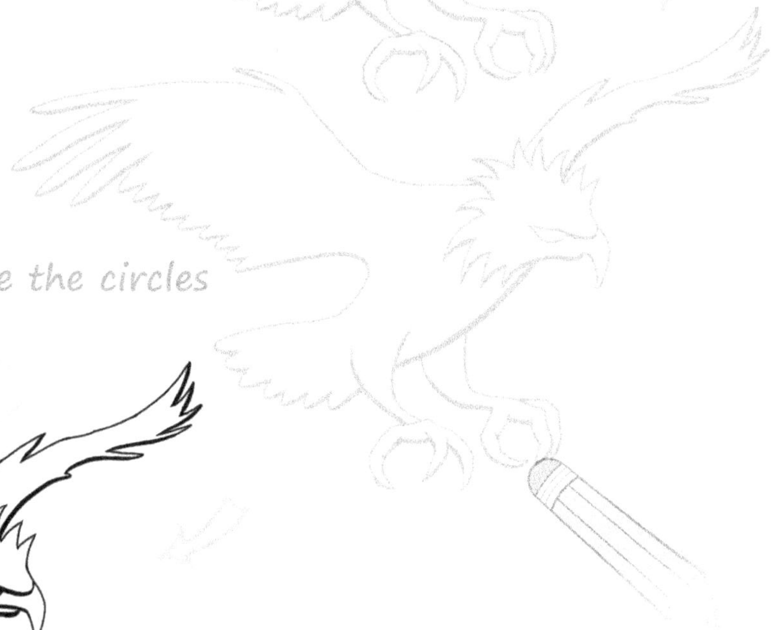

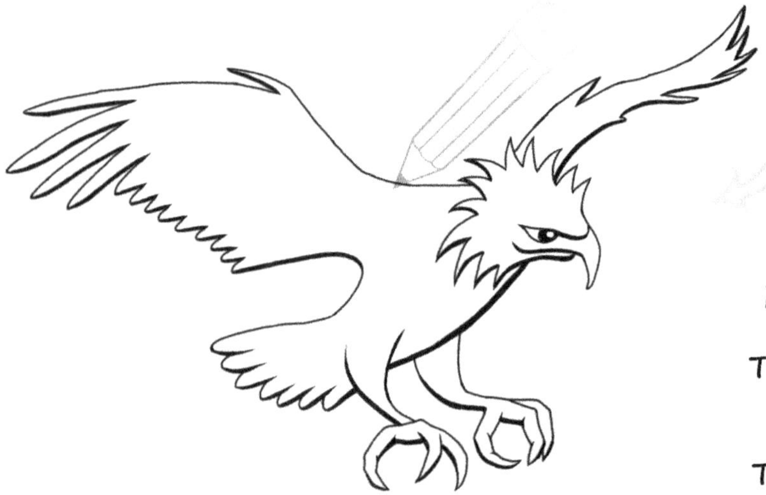

STEP 4 – FINISH:
Add details, Draw dark

DRAWING TIPS:

Try drawing some lines thick,
and other lines thin.

Try drawing different shaped eyes

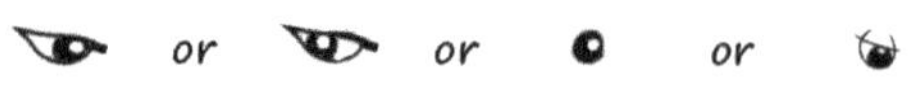

or   or   or

Philippine Eagle

Use this as a guide
for each of the
steps in creating
your own drawing.

Fun Facts:

Philippine Eagle

Reasons for Endangerment:
1. Deforestation: Their homes in the rainforest are being cut down for logging and to clear land for farming.
2. Hunting: They are sometimes killed by people who see them as a threat to their livestock or for illegal wildlife trade.
3. Pesticides: Chemicals used in farming can poison the animals they eat, which can then make the eagles sick.

Population in the Wild:
• Very few, estimated to be around 400 pairs left in the wild.

Population in Captivity:
• A small number are in conservation centers and zoos, primarily in the Philippines, where breeding and conservation programs are ongoing.

Countries/Areas of Natural Habitat:
• Found only in the Philippines, mainly in the remaining patches of rainforest on islands like Luzon, Leyte, Samar, and Mindanao.

Interesting Facts:
1. Impressive Size: They are one of the largest eagles in the world, with a wingspan of up to 7 feet and very powerful talons.
2. Monogamous Birds: They mate for life and are known to share parenting duties, taking turns looking after their eggs and hunting for food.
3. National Symbol: The Philippine eagle is the national bird of the Philippines, symbolizing strength and freedom.

STEP 1 - START:
Draw light circles

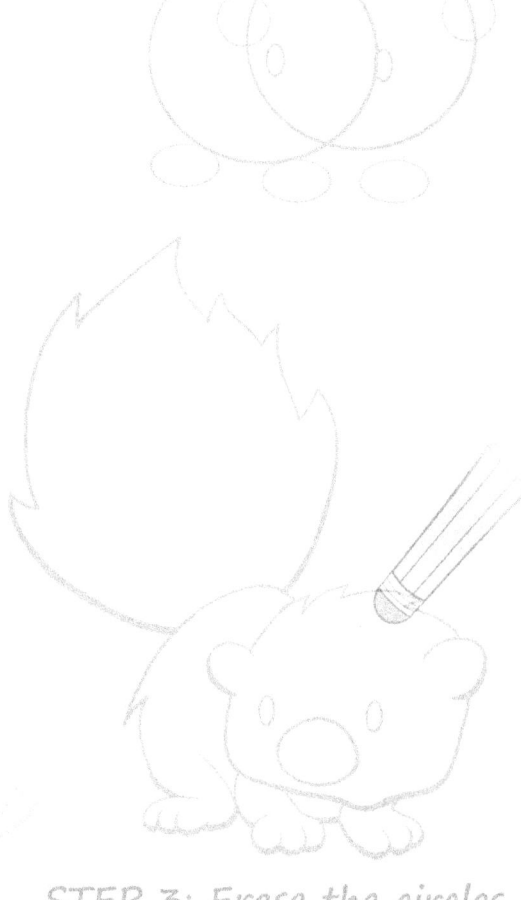

STEP 2: Draw light lines

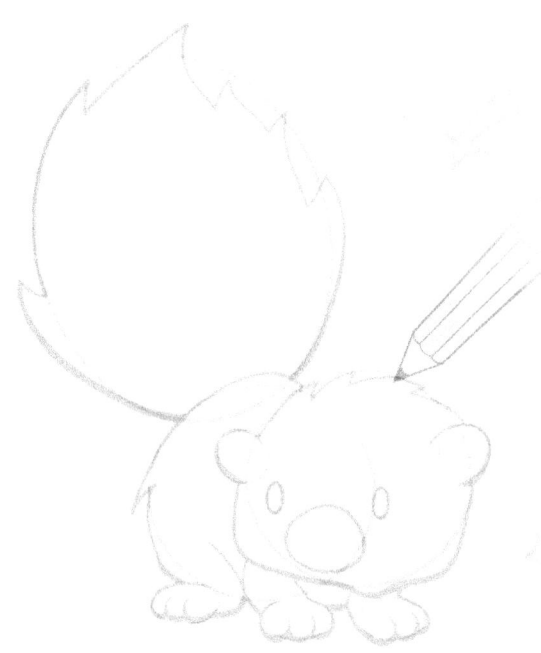

STEP 3: Erase the circles

STEP 4 - FINISH:
Add details, Draw dark

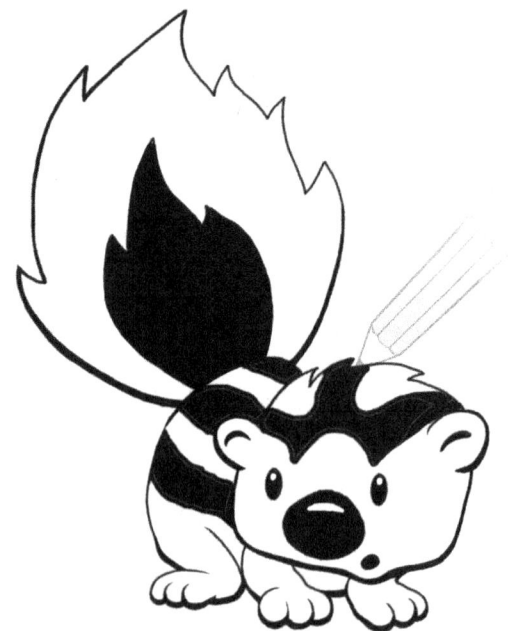

DRAWING TIPS:

Try drawing some lines thick,
and other lines thin.

Try drawing different shaped eyes

  or

Eastern Spotted Skunk

Use this as a guide
for each of the
steps in creating
your own drawing.

Fun Facts:

Eastern Spotted Skunk

Reasons for Endangerment:
  1. Habitat Loss: Their homes in forests and grasslands are being changed into farms or places for people to live.
  2. Pesticides: Chemicals used on farms can poison the insects and small animals they eat.
  3. Predation and Human Conflict: They are sometimes hunted by predators or people who consider them pests.
Population in the Wild:
  • Not well-known, but their numbers are believed to be decreasing.
Population in Captivity:
  • Rarely found in captivity as they are wild animals that thrive best in their natural environment.
Countries/Areas of Natural Habitat:
  • Found in eastern parts of the United States, from Canada down to the Gulf of Mexico.
Interesting Facts:
  1. Distinctive Stripes: They have white spots and broken stripes against their black fur, which makes them
      stand out from other skunk species.
  2. Impressive Acrobat: When threatened, they can perform a handstand to show off their warning colors and
      spray better if they need to.
  3. Omnivorous Diet: They eat a varied diet, including insects, small mammals, birds, eggs, and fruits.

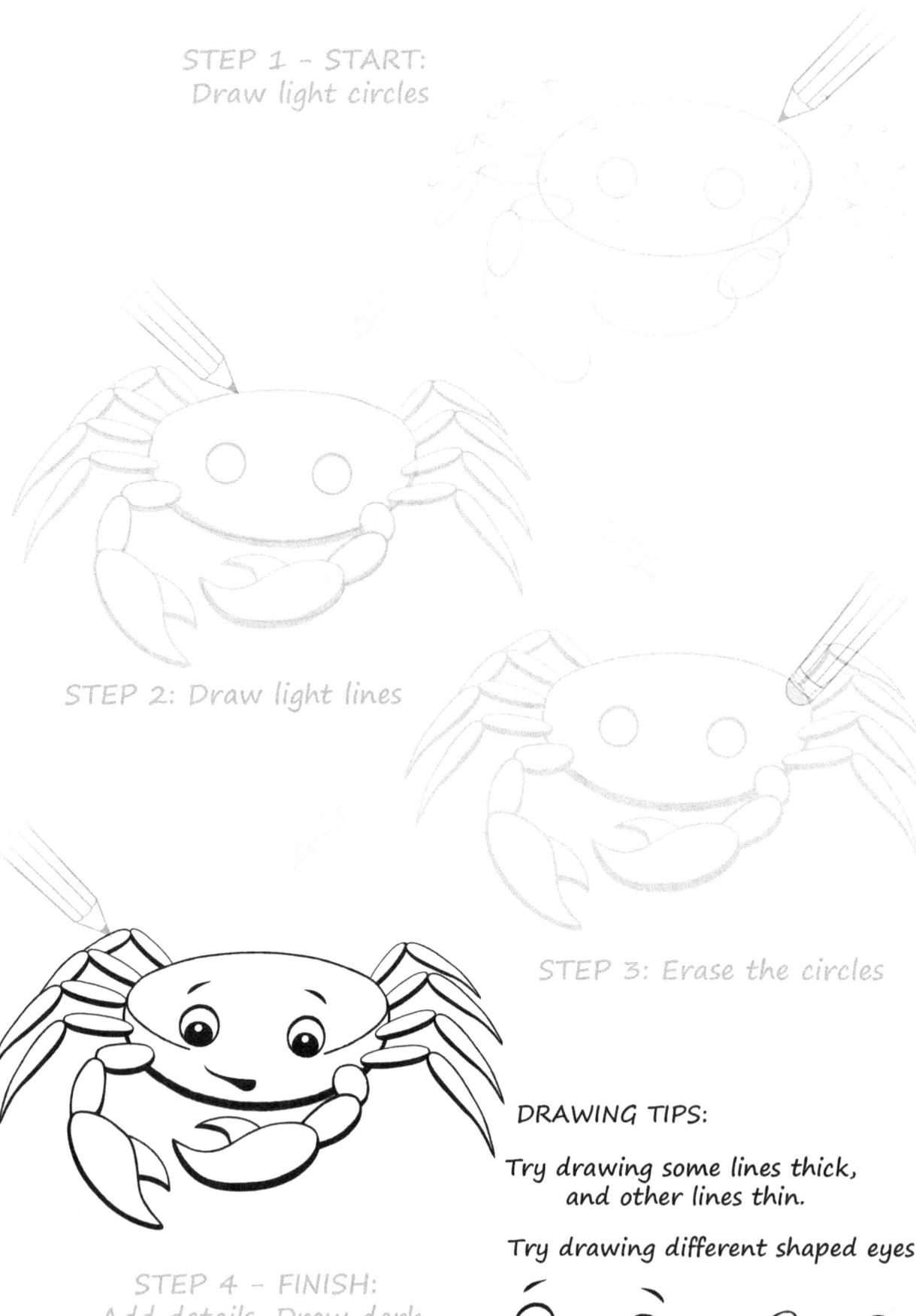

STEP 1 – START:
Draw light circles

STEP 2: Draw light lines

STEP 3: Erase the circles

STEP 4 – FINISH:
Add details, Draw dark

DRAWING TIPS:

Try drawing some lines thick,
and other lines thin.

Try drawing different shaped eyes

or

Giri Putri Cave Crab

Fun Facts:

Giri Putri Cave Crab

Reasons for Endangerment:
1. Limited Habitat: They live only in a specific cave system, so any changes or damage to this habitat can have a big impact on their population.
2. Human Disturbance: The caves where they live can be disturbed by tourists and other human activities.
3. Pollution: Pollution from outside sources can get into the caves and harm the delicate ecosystem they rely on.

Population in the Wild:
• Not well-known, but believed to be very limited due to their restricted habitat.

Population in Captivity:
• Not typically found in captivity because of their specific and sensitive habitat requirements.

Countries/Areas of Natural Habitat:
• Found only in the Giri Putri Cave on Nusa Penida Island, part of Bali, Indonesia.

Interesting Facts:
1. Cave Dwellers: They are specially adapted to live in the dark, humid environment of the Giri Putri Cave.
2. Rare and Unique: They are one of the few species of crabs that live exclusively in a cave environment, making them very unique.
3. Important for the Ecosystem: As part of the cave's ecosystem, they help recycle nutrients and keep the environment balanced.

Use this as a guide for each of the steps in creating your own drawing.

STEP 1 – START:
Draw light circles

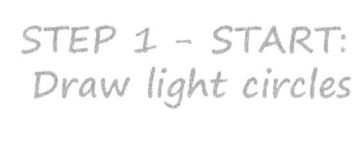

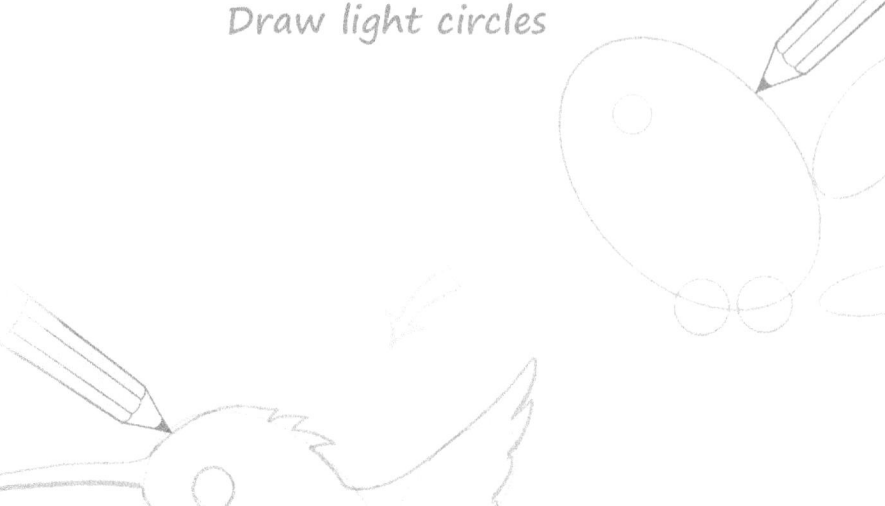

STEP 2: Draw light lines

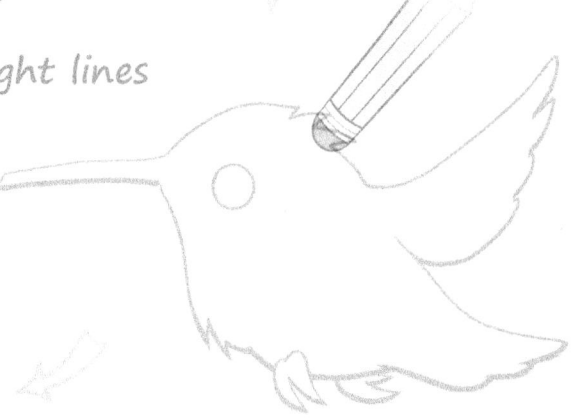

STEP 3: Erase the circles

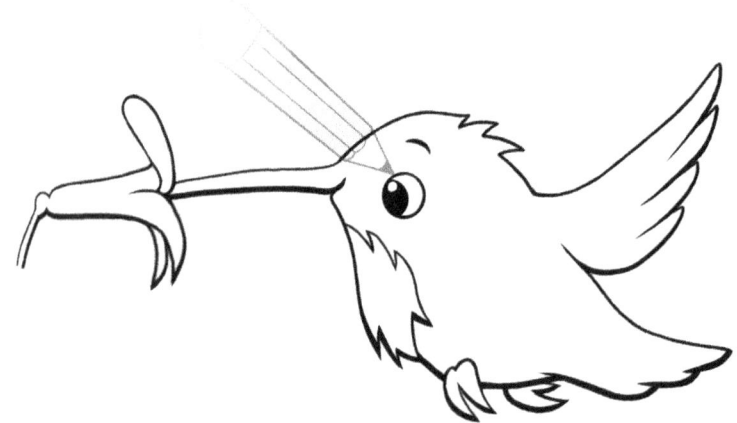

STEP 4 – FINISH:
Add details, Draw dark

DRAWING TIPS:

Try drawing some lines thick,
and other lines thin.

Try drawing different shaped eyes

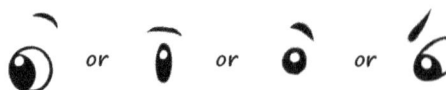

Gorgeted Puffleg Hummingbird

Use this as a guide
for each of the
steps in creating
your own drawing.

Fun Facts:

Gorgeted Puffleg Hummingbird

Reasons for Endangerment:
   1. Habitat Loss: Their homes in the forests are being cut down for farming or building houses.
   2. Climate Change: Changes in the weather are affecting the flowers they need for food.
Population in the Wild:
   • Very few, estimated to be between 250 and 999 adult birds.
Population in Captivity:
   • Not commonly found in captivity.
Countries/Areas of Natural Habitat:
   • Lives in the cloud forests of Colombia, South America.
Interesting Facts:
   1. Sparkling Throat: The males have a shiny throat patch called a 'gorget', which looks like a glittering necklace.
   2. Fast Flyers: They can flap their wings super fast, about 80 times per second!
   3. Important Pollinators: They help flowers grow by carrying pollen from one flower to another while they sip nectar.

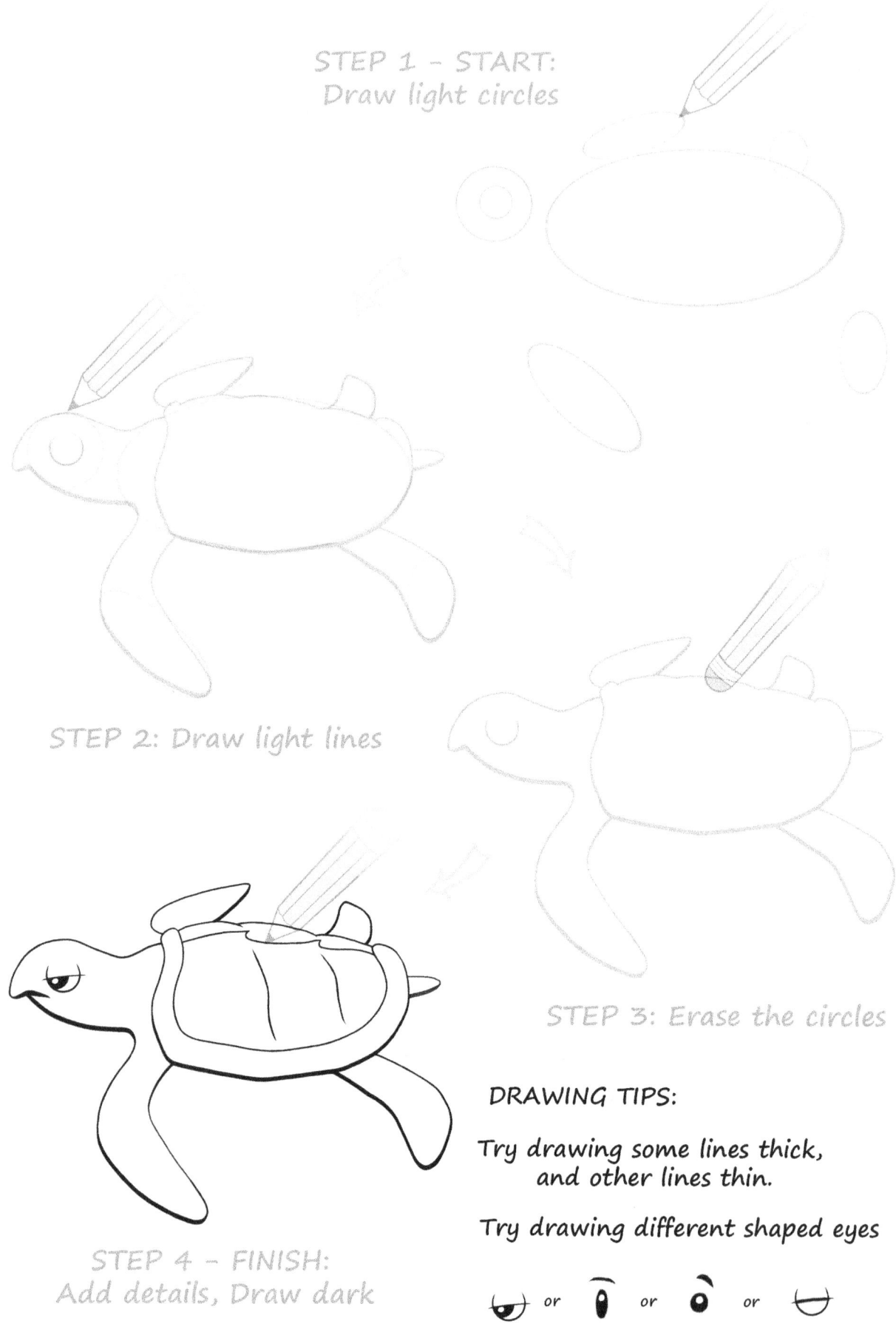

STEP 1 – START:
Draw light circles

STEP 2: Draw light lines

STEP 3: Erase the circles

STEP 4 – FINISH:
Add details, Draw dark

DRAWING TIPS:

Try drawing some lines thick,
and other lines thin.

Try drawing different shaped eyes

Kemp's Ridley Sea Turtle

Fun Facts:

Kemp's Ridley Sea Turtle

Use this as a guide for each of the steps in creating your own drawing.

Reasons for Endangerment:
1. Egg Poaching: Their eggs are often taken from beaches by people who sell them or eat them.
2. Accidental Capture: They can get caught in fishing nets or on hooks, which can hurt them or make it hard for them to swim and find food.
3. Pollution: Trash, oil spills, and chemicals in the water can make them sick and pollute the beaches where they lay their eggs.

Population in the Wild:
- Estimated to be around 7,000-9,000 nesting females, but their numbers have been increasing due to conservation efforts.

Population in Captivity:
- Some are in rescue and rehabilitation centers, especially those affected by oil spills or injuries, but they are not typically kept in long-term captivity.

Countries/Areas of Natural Habitat:
- Mostly found in the Gulf of Mexico, but they also live in the Atlantic Ocean and can be seen along the coasts of the United States and Mexico.

Interesting Facts:
1. Smallest Sea Turtle: Kemp's Ridley is the smallest of the sea turtles, with adults weighing about 100 pounds.
2. Unique Nesting: They have a unique nesting behavior called "arribada," where thousands of females come to the same beach to lay eggs at the same time.
3. Strong Swimmers: Despite their small size, they are powerful swimmers and travel long distances to find food and nesting sites.

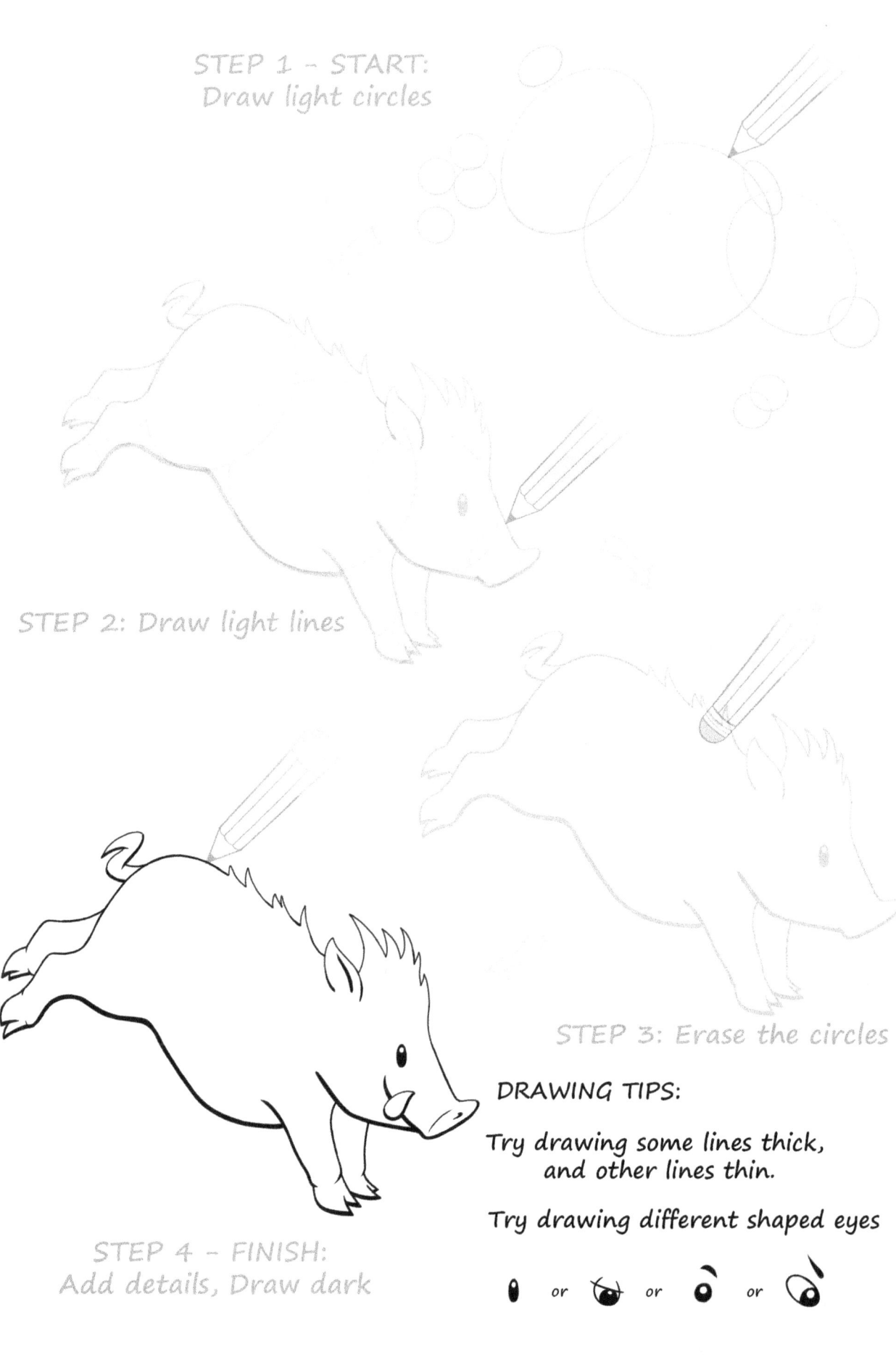

STEP 1 - START:
Draw light circles

STEP 2: Draw light lines

STEP 3: Erase the circles

STEP 4 - FINISH:
Add details, Draw dark

DRAWING TIPS:

Try drawing some lines thick,
and other lines thin.

Try drawing different shaped eyes

or   or   or

Visayan Warty Pig

Use this as a guide
for each of the
steps in creating
your own drawing.

Fun Facts:

Visayan Warty Pig

Reasons for Endangerment:
  1. Losing Their Home: People are cutting down the forests where they live to make room for farms and houses.
  2. Hunted for Food: Some people hunt them for food, even though it's not allowed.
  3. Competing for Food: They have to compete with domestic animals for the food that's available in their habitat.

Population in the Wild:
  • Very few left, estimated to be fewer than 200.

Population in Captivity:
  • Around 200 in zoos and breeding centers to help increase their numbers.

Countries/Areas of Natural Habitat:
  • They used to roam around many islands in the Philippines, but now they are mostly found on the Visayan Islands.

Interesting Facts:
  1. Unique Hairdo: The males have a cool mohawk-like mane of hair that stands up when they are excited.
  2. Warty Face: They get their name from the three pairs of warts on their faces. Scientists think these might help protect their face when they fight.
  3. Super Sniffers: They have an excellent sense of smell, which helps them find food hidden underground.

STEP 1 - START:
Draw light circles

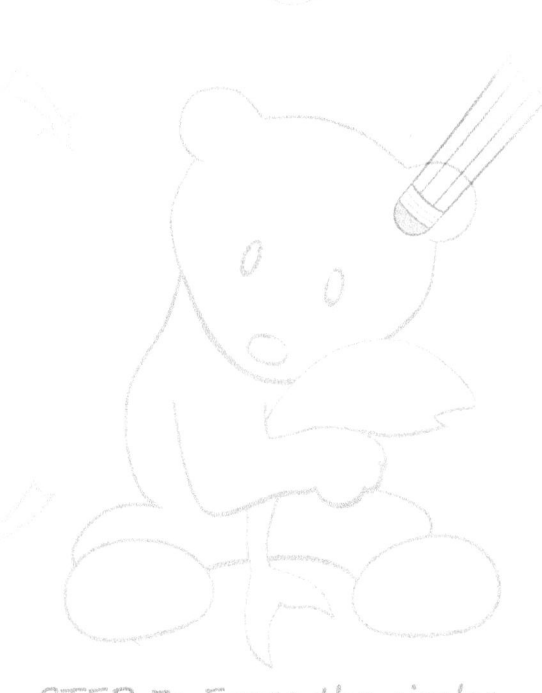

STEP 2: Draw light lines

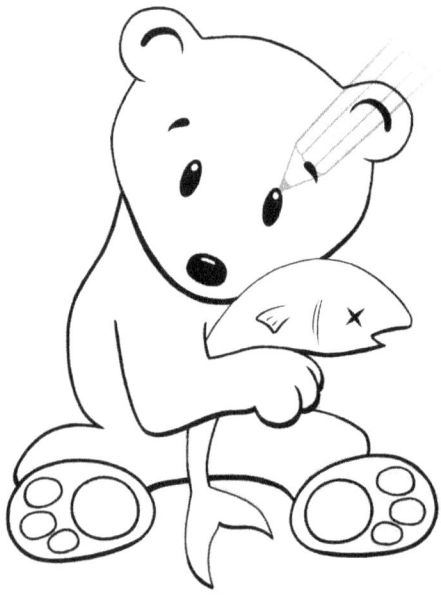

STEP 3: Erase the circles

STEP 4 - FINISH:
Add details, Draw dark

DRAWING TIPS:

Try drawing some lines thick,
and other lines thin.

Try drawing different shaped eyes

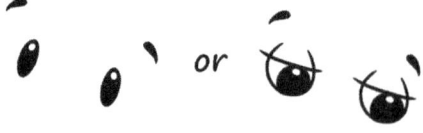 or

Asiatic Black Bear Cub

Use this as a guide
for each of the
steps in creating
your own drawing.

Fun Facts:

Asiatic Black Bear

Reasons for Endangerment:
1. Habitat Loss: Their forest homes are being cut down, making it hard for them to find food and shelter.
2. Hunted for Body Parts: Some people hunt them for their body parts, which are wrongly believed to be good for health.
3. Human Conflict: Sometimes they wander into human areas looking for food, which can lead to trouble.

Population in the Wild:
• Estimated to be around 50,000, but numbers are decreasing.

Population in Captivity:
• Not commonly kept in captivity, mostly found in rescue centers or wildlife sanctuaries.

Countries/Areas of Natural Habitat:
• Found in forests across Asia, including countries like China, India, Russia, and Japan.

Interesting Facts:
1. Tree Climbers: They are excellent at climbing trees and often sleep or hide in trees for safety.
2. Winter Nap: They hibernate during the winter, sleeping in dens for months without eating.
3. Omnivores: They eat a mixed diet, enjoying fruits, nuts, insects, and sometimes even small animals.

STEP 1 – START:
Draw light circles

STEP 2: Draw light lines

STEP 3: Erase the circles

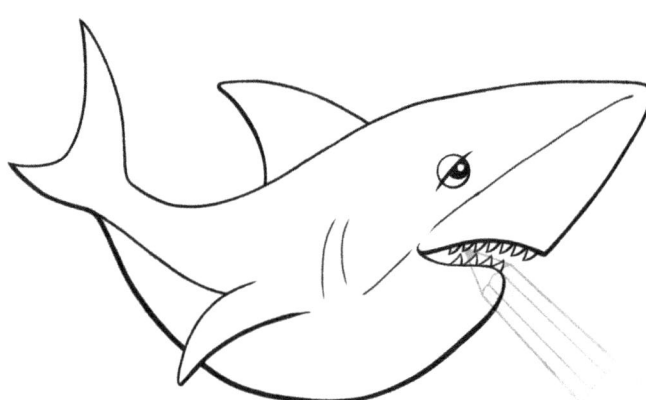

STEP 4 – FINISH:
Add details, Draw dark

DRAWING TIPS:

Try drawing some lines thick,
and other lines thin.

Try drawing different shaped eyes

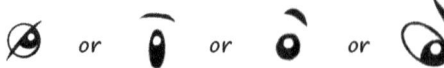

Great White Shark

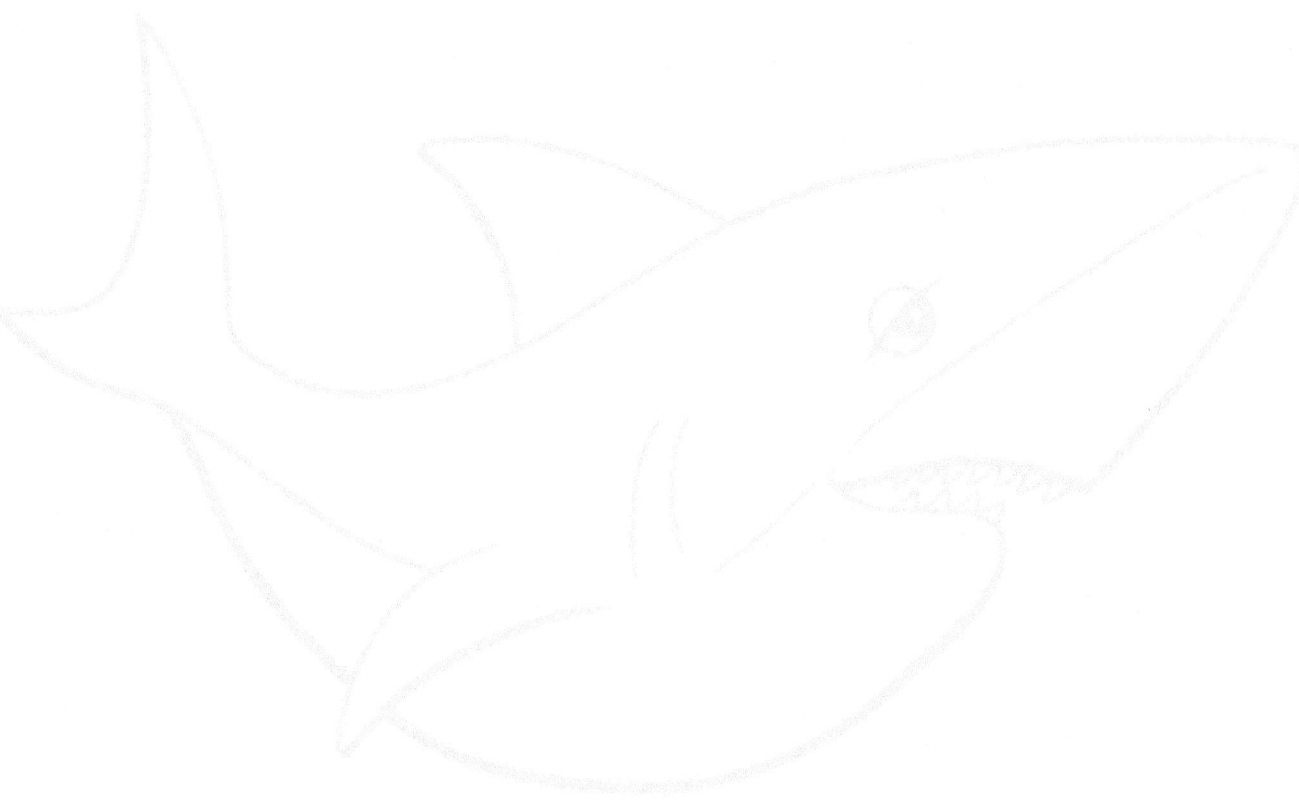

Use this as a guide for each of the steps in creating your own drawing.

Fun Facts:

Great White Shark

Reasons for Endangerment:
  1. Overfishing: They get caught in fishing nets or on hooks, even though people aren't always trying to catch them.
  2. Hunted for Their Parts: Some people hunt them for their fins, teeth, and jaws, which are used in souvenirs or medicines.
  3. Pollution: Their ocean home is getting dirty with things like plastic and chemicals, which can make them sick.
Population in the Wild:
  • Exact numbers are unknown, but they are considered a vulnerable species.
Population in Captivity:
  • Very rare in captivity as they do not survive well in aquariums.
Countries/Areas of Natural Habitat:
  • Found in cool, coastal waters all around the world, especially off the coasts of the United States, South Africa, Japan, and Australia.
Interesting Facts:
  1. Big Swimmers: They can swim very long distances, even from one country to another!
  2. Built-in GPS: They have an excellent sense of direction and can find their way through vast oceans.
  3. Powerful Hunters: They are at the top of the food chain and are known for their strength, speed, and sharp teeth.

STEP 1 – START:
Draw light circles

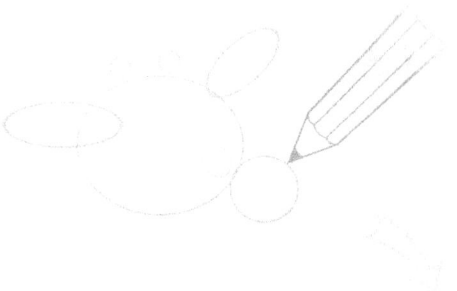

STEP 2: Draw light lines

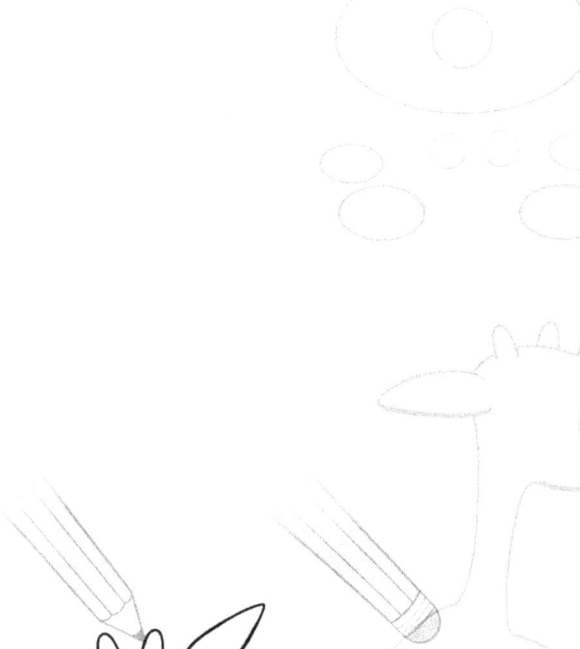

STEP 3: Erase the circles

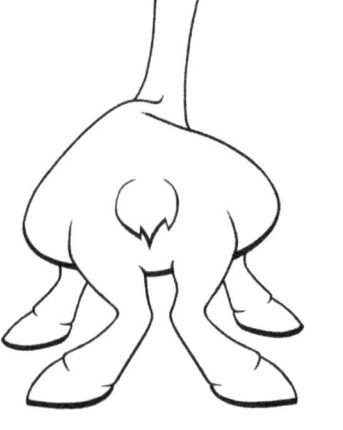

STEP 4 – FINISH:
Add details, Draw dark

DRAWING TIPS:

Try drawing some lines thick,
and other lines thin.

Try drawing different shaped eyes

 or or or

Arapawa Goat

Use this as a guide
for each of the
steps in creating
your own drawing.

Fun Facts:

Arapawa Goat

Reasons for Endangerment:
1. Loss of Habitat: Their living areas are getting smaller as people use the land for building or farming.
2. Competition for Food: They have to share their food with other animals, which sometimes leaves not enough for them.
3. Hunting and Disease: Sometimes people hunt them, and they can also get sick from diseases.

Population in the Wild:
• A small number, mostly living on Arapawa Island in New Zealand.

Population in Captivity:
• A few hundred in various parts of the world, mainly kept by breeders trying to protect them.

Countries/Areas of Natural Habitat:
• Originally from Arapawa Island in New Zealand. Some have been taken to other countries to help protect the breed.

Interesting Facts:
1. Unique Look: They have a distinct appearance with long, twisted horns and a variety of coat colors.
2. Survival Skills: They are known for being tough and can survive in harsh conditions where other goats might not.
3. Historical Mystery: It's not completely clear how they got to Arapawa Island. Some think they were left there by sailors many years ago!

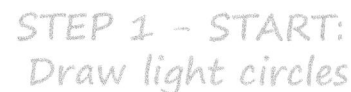

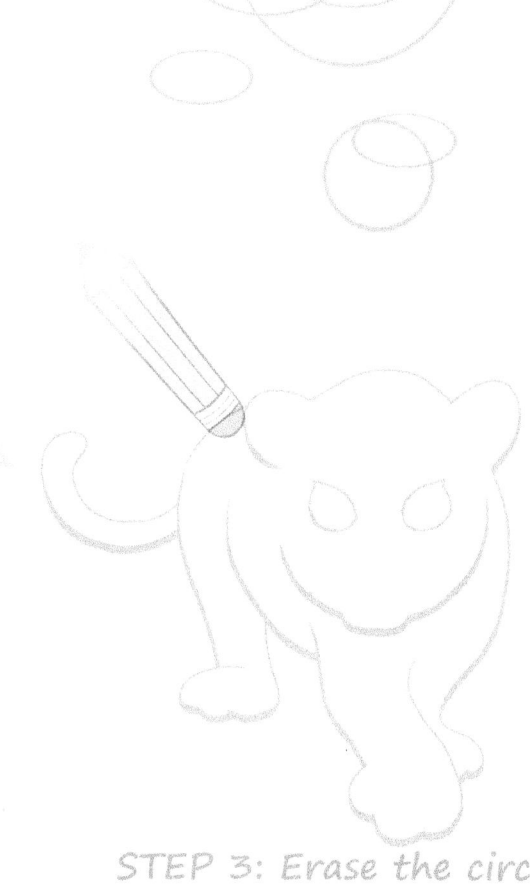

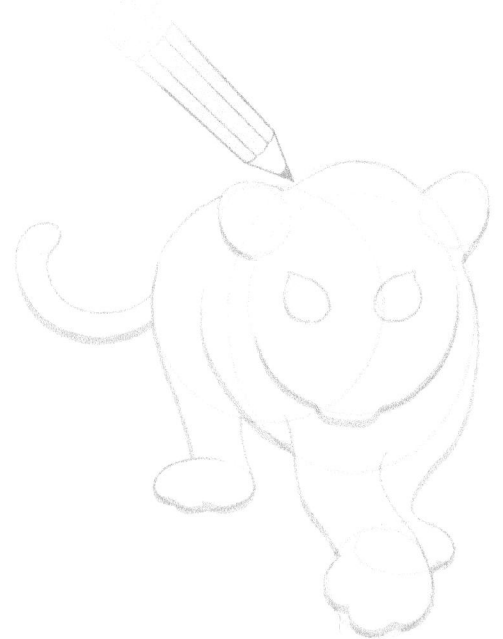

STEP 2: Draw light lines

STEP 3: Erase the circles

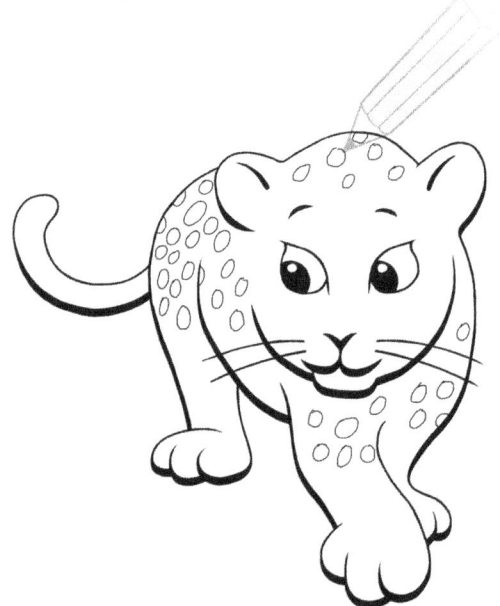

STEP 4 – FINISH:
Add details, Draw dark

DRAWING TIPS:

Try drawing some lines thick,
and other lines thin.

Try drawing different shaped eyes

    or

Amur Leopard

Use this as a guide
for each of the
steps in creating
your own drawing.

Fun Facts:

Amur Leopard

Reasons for Endangerment:
1. Habitat Loss: Their homes in the forest are being cut down for timber and to make room for farming and human settlements.
2. Poaching: Some people illegally hunt them for their beautiful fur and body parts.
3. Food Shortage: They are having a hard time finding enough food because their prey is also getting less common due to habitat loss and other factors.

Population in the Wild:
• Very few, around 100 known to exist in the wild as of the latest counts.

Population in Captivity:
• About 200 in zoos worldwide, where breeding programs are helping to increase their numbers.

Countries/Areas of Natural Habitat:
• Mainly found in the Russian Far East and China, in temperate, broadleaf, and mixed forests.

Interesting Facts:
1. Incredible Climbers: They are fantastic at climbing trees, and they often rest on tree branches during the day.
2. Solo Lifestyle: They are solitary creatures, living and hunting alone most of the time.
3. Fast and Strong: They can run at speeds of up to 37 miles per hour, and they can carry prey up to three times their own weight up into the trees.

STEP 1 – START:
Draw light circles

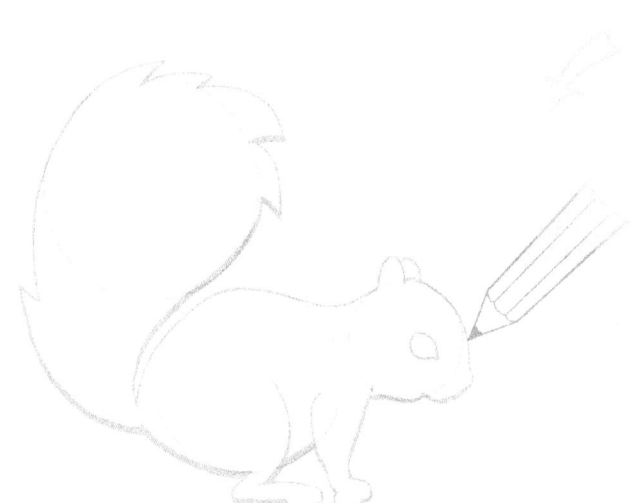

STEP 2: Draw light lines

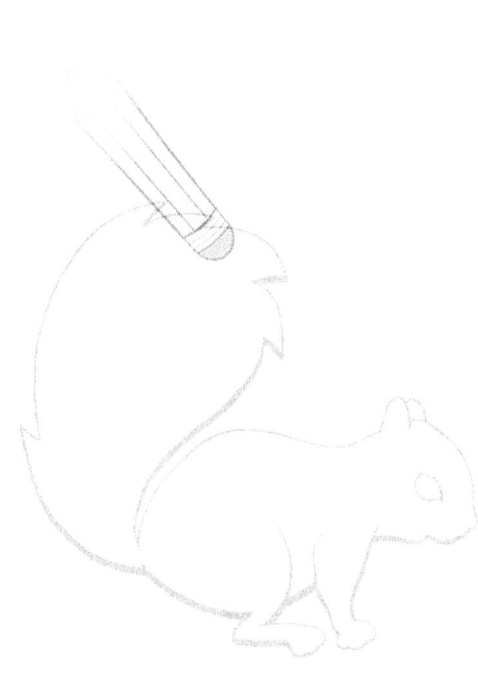

STEP 3: Erase the circles

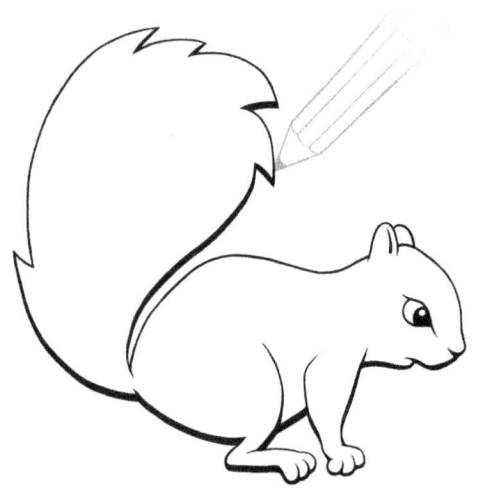

STEP 4 – FINISH:
Add details, Draw dark

DRAWING TIPS:

Try drawing some lines thick,
and other lines thin.

Try drawing different shaped eyes

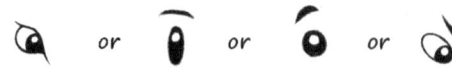

Western Gray Squirrel

Use this as a guide for each of the steps in creating your own drawing.

Fun Facts:

Western Gray Squirrel

Reasons for Endangerment:
1. Habitat Loss: Their homes in oak woodlands and conifer forests are being cut down or changed into places for people to live.
2. Competition for Food and Space: They have to compete with other animals, like the Eastern Gray Squirrel, for food and places to live.
3. Diseases and Predation: They can get sick from diseases and are also hunted by predators like hawks and foxes.

Population in the Wild:
• Their numbers are decreasing, but they are still found in certain areas, especially in the western United States.

Population in Captivity:
• Not commonly kept in captivity, as they are wild animals that thrive best in their natural habitat.

Countries/Areas of Natural Habitat:
• Mainly found in the western United States, particularly in states like California, Washington, and Oregon.

Interesting Facts:
1. Big and Fluffy: They are one of the largest types of tree squirrels in the United States, known for their bushy tails and gray fur.
2. Great Jumpers: They can leap from tree to tree and are very agile when searching for food or escaping predators.
3. Forest Gardeners: By burying nuts and not finding all of them, they help plant new trees, helping the forest grow.

STEP 1 – START:
Draw light circles

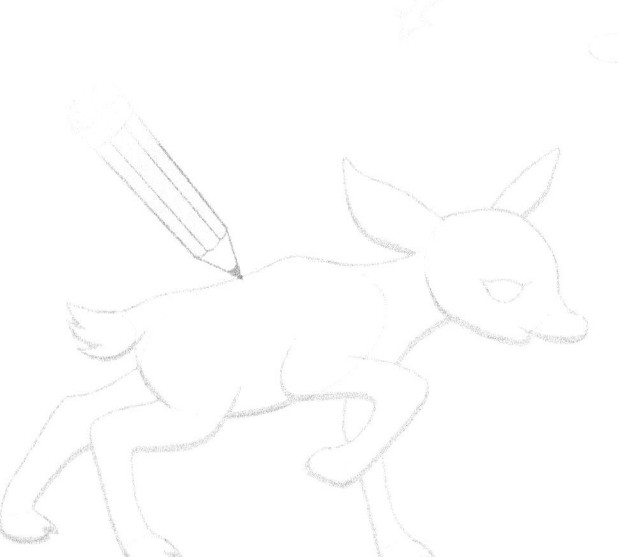

STEP 2: Draw light lines

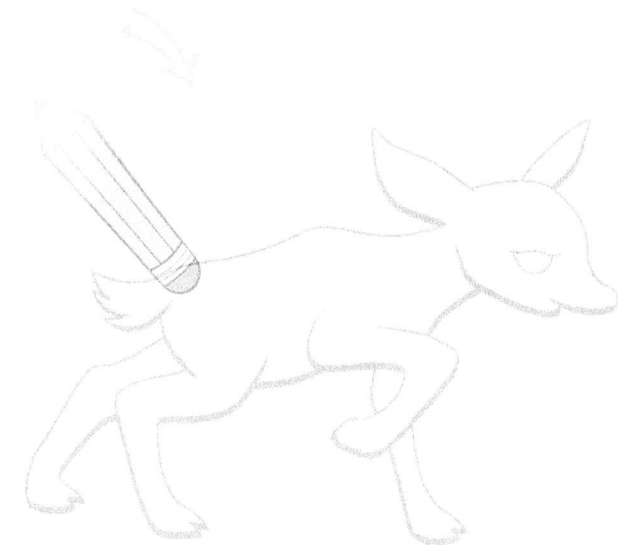

STEP 3: Erase the circles

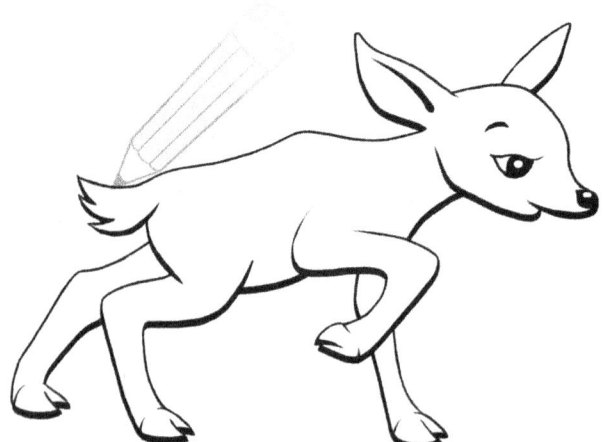

STEP 4 – FINISH:
Add details, Draw dark

DRAWING TIPS:

Try drawing some lines thick,
and other lines thin.

Try drawing different shaped eyes

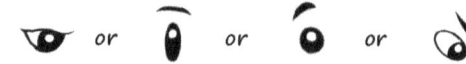

Key Deer

Use this as a guide for each of the steps in creating your own drawing.

Fun Facts:

Key Deer

Reasons for Endangerment:
1. Habitat Loss: Their living space in the Florida Keys is being taken over by people building homes and roads.
2. Car Accidents: Many are hit by cars because they live close to roads and sometimes cross them.
3. Hurricanes and Climate Change: Storms and rising sea levels can damage the places where they live and find food.

Population in the Wild:
• Around 600 to 800, but their numbers can change due to threats like habitat loss and hurricanes.

Population in Captivity:
• Not commonly kept in captivity. Conservation efforts focus on protecting them in their natural habitat.

Countries/Areas of Natural Habitat:
• Found only in the Florida Keys, a group of islands off the coast of Florida, USA.

Interesting Facts:
1. Tiny Deer: The Key deer is the smallest subspecies of North American white-tailed deer, about the size of a big dog.
2. Swimming Skills: They are good swimmers and can move between islands in the Florida Keys.
3. Friendly Nature: They are known to be quite friendly and sometimes even approach people, but it's important to remember not to feed them or disturb their natural behavior.

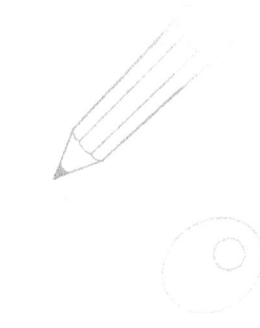

STEP 2: Draw light lines

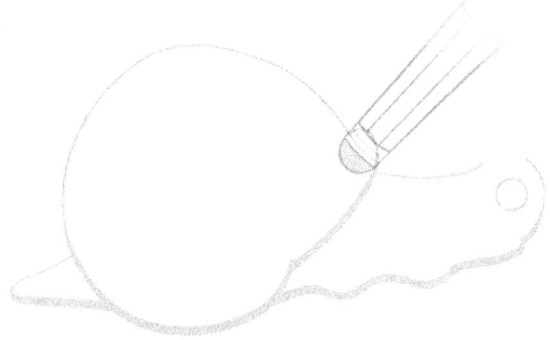

STEP 3: Erase the circles

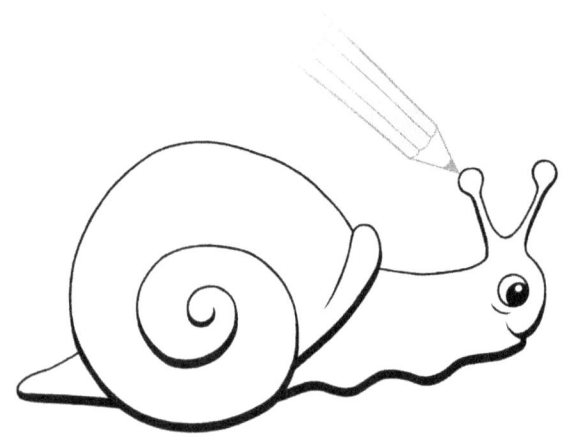

STEP 4 – FINISH:
Add details, Draw dark

DRAWING TIPS:

Try drawing some lines thick,
and other lines thin.

Try drawing different shaped eyes

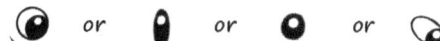

Powelliphanta Snail

Use this as a guide
for each of the
steps in creating
your own drawing.

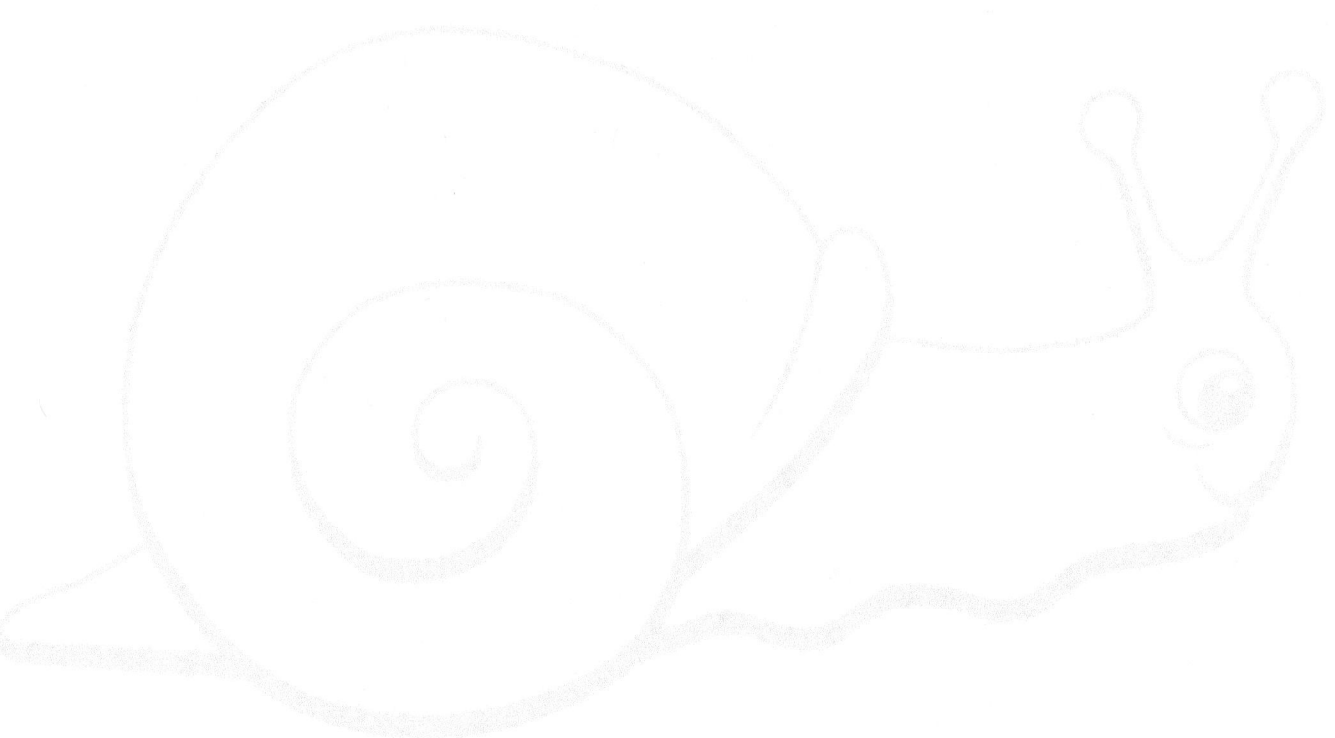

Fun Facts:

Powelliphanta Snail

Reasons for Endangerment:
1. Habitat Loss: Their forest homes are being changed into land for farms or houses, leaving them with fewer places to live.
2. Predators: Animals like rats and possums, which were brought to New Zealand by people, like to eat these snails.
3. Pollution and Climate Change: Changes in weather and pollution can harm the places where they live and find food.

Population in the Wild:
• Not exactly known, but many species of Powelliphanta snails are considered to be at risk or threatened.

Population in Captivity:
• Very rare in captivity, mainly because they require specific conditions that are hard to recreate outside their natural habitat.

Countries/Areas of Natural Habitat:
• Found only in New Zealand, especially in native forests and alpine grasslands.

Interesting Facts:
1. Giant Snails: They are one of the largest snail species in the world, with some shells being as big as a person's hand!
2. Carnivorous Diet: Unlike most snails that eat plants, Powelliphanta snails are carnivorous, which means they eat meat, like worms and other small invertebrates.
3. Beautiful Shells: They have strikingly patterned shells, which make them not only fascinating creatures but also beautiful to look at.

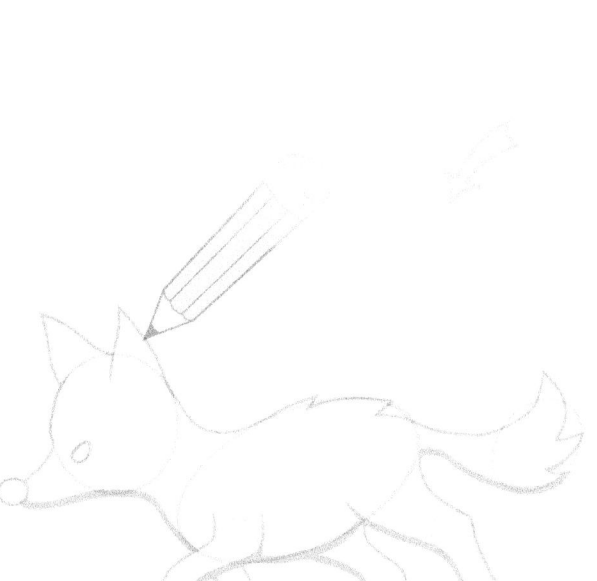

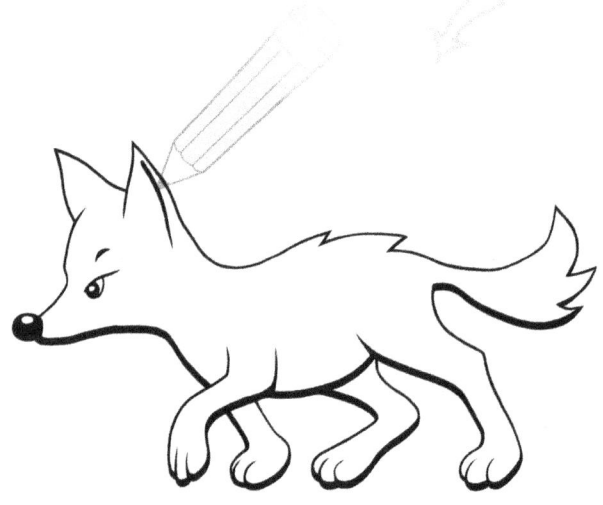

DRAWING TIPS:

Try drawing some lines thick,
and other lines thin.

Try drawing different shaped eyes

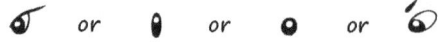

Sierra Nevada Gray Fox

Use this as a guide for each of the steps in creating your own drawing.

Fun Facts:

Sierra Nevada Gray Fox

Reasons for Endangerment:
1. Habitat Loss: Their homes in the forests are being cut down or changed by people building things or using the land for other reasons.
2. Food Shortage: They find it hard to get enough food when their habitat is disturbed or when there are fewer small animals for them to eat.
3. Competition and Predation: They have to compete with other animals for food, and sometimes they are hunted by larger predators.

Population in the Wild:
• Not exactly known, but they are considered less common than other types of foxes.

Population in Captivity:
• Rarely found in captivity as they are very elusive and prefer living in the wild.

Countries/Areas of Natural Habitat:
• Found in the Sierra Nevada mountain range and other mountainous areas in California, USA.

Interesting Facts:
1. Tree Climbers: Unlike many other types of foxes, the Sierra Nevada Gray Fox can climb trees to find food or escape from predators.
2. Nocturnal Creatures: They are most active at night, which is when they hunt for small animals like rodents and rabbits.
3. Beautiful Coats: They have a distinctive salt-and-pepper gray coat, with a black stripe running down their back and a bushy tail with a black tip.

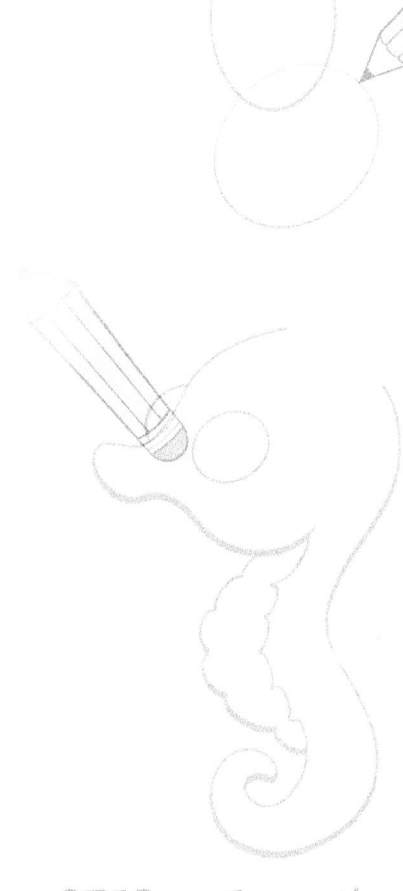

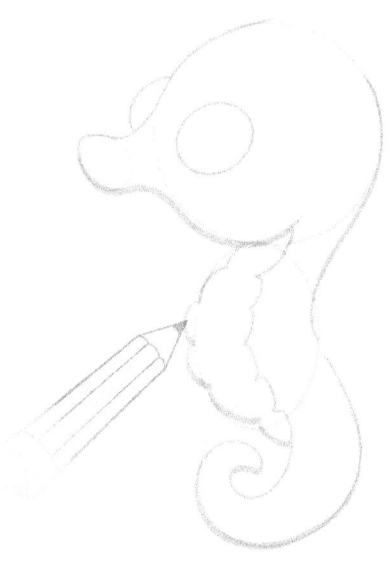

STEP 2: Draw light lines

STEP 3: Erase the circles

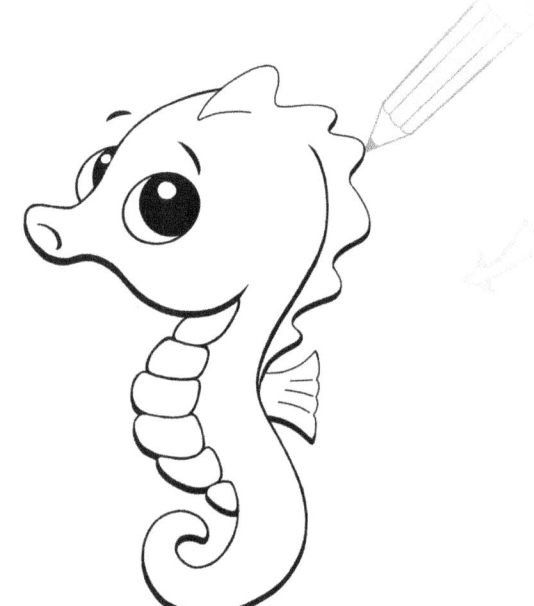

STEP 4 – FINISH:
Add details, Draw dark

DRAWING TIPS:

Try drawing some lines thick,
and other lines thin.

Try drawing different shaped eyes

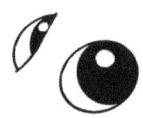 or

Cape Seahorse

Use this as a guide
for each of the
steps in creating
your own drawing.

Fun Facts:

Cape Seahorse

Reasons for Endangerment:
1. Habitat Destruction: Their homes in the underwater plants and coral reefs are being damaged or destroyed by pollution and changing sea conditions.
2. Fishing: They sometimes get caught in fishing nets by accident. Also, some people catch them to sell as pets or use in traditional medicines.
3. Pollution: Water pollution from land, like trash and chemicals, can make them sick and harm the places where they live.

Population in the Wild:
• Not exactly known, but their numbers are believed to be decreasing.

Population in Captivity:
• Some are kept in aquariums and marine parks, and they are also bred in captivity to help protect the wild population.

Countries/Areas of Natural Habitat:
• Found in the coastal waters of South Africa, especially around the Cape of Good Hope.

Interesting Facts:
1. Dad Carries the Babies: Unlike most animals, the male seahorse carries the eggs in a pouch until they hatch.
2. Masters of Camouflage: They are really good at blending in with their surroundings to hide from predators.
3. Unique Swimmers: They swim upright and use their small fins to steer through the water.

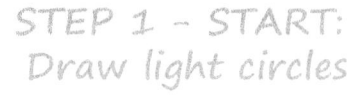

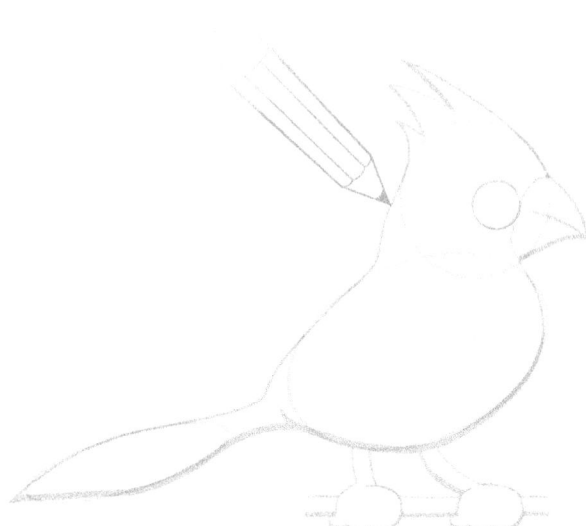

STEP 2: Draw light lines

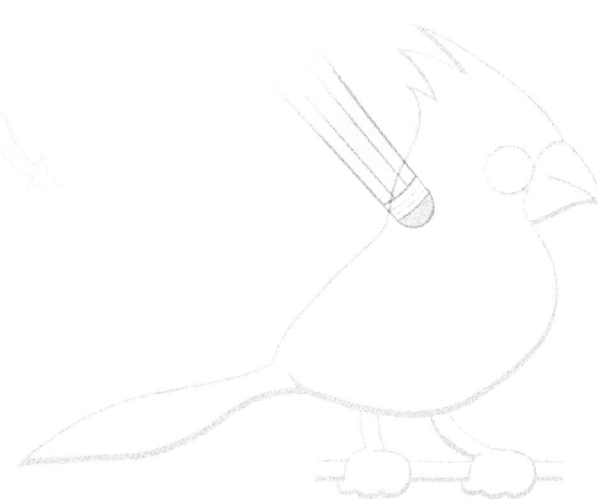

STEP 3: Erase the circles

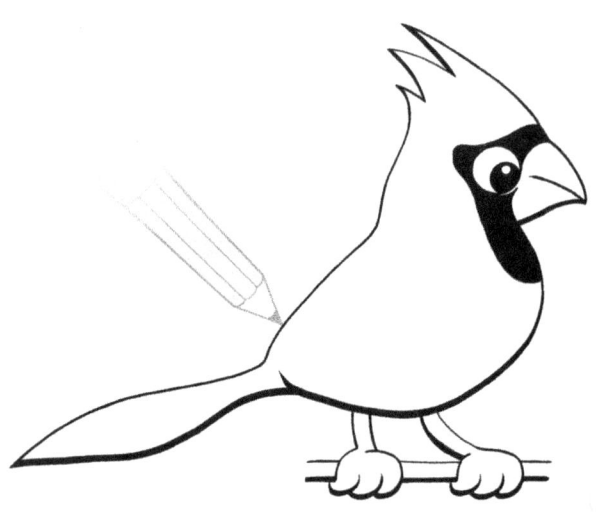

STEP 4 – FINISH:
Add details, Draw dark

DRAWING TIPS:

Try drawing some lines thick,
and other lines thin.

Try drawing different shaped eyes

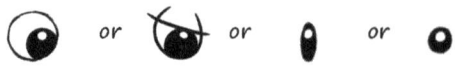

Yellow Cardinal

Use this as a guide for each of the steps in creating your own drawing.

Fun Facts:

Yellow Cardinal

Reasons for Endangerment:
1. Trapped for Pets: Many are caught and sold as pets because people like their beautiful singing and bright color.
2. Habitat Loss: The places where they live, like grasslands and open woodlands, are being changed into farms or cities.
3. Nest Robbing: Sometimes, their eggs or baby birds are taken from their nests.

Population in the Wild:
• Very few, estimated to be only a few thousand left.

Population in Captivity:
• More common in captivity due to their popularity as pets, but this is also a problem for their wild population.

Countries/Areas of Natural Habitat:
• Mainly found in parts of South America, like Argentina, Uruguay, Paraguay, and southern Brazil.

Interesting Facts:
1. Sunny Singers: Known for their beautiful and strong singing voice, which can be heard especially during the breeding season.
2. Bright and Beautiful: Males have a striking yellow color with a black throat, which makes them easy to spot.
3. Shy and Secretive: They are quite elusive in the wild, preferring to stay hidden in dense shrubs and trees.

STEP 1 – START:
Draw light circles

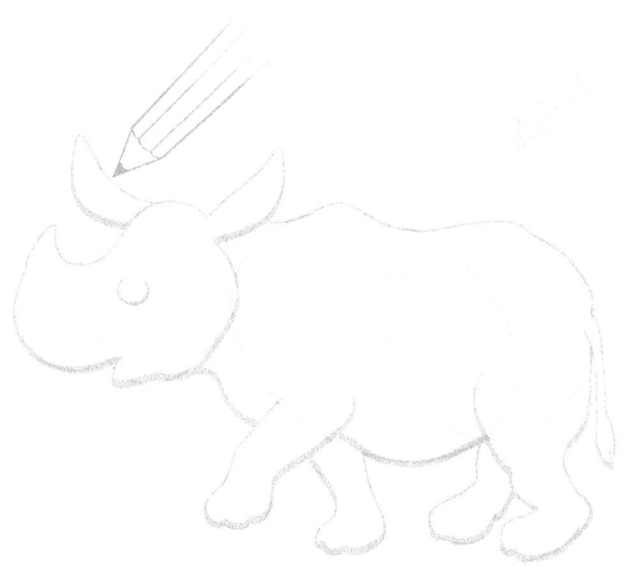

STEP 2: Draw light lines

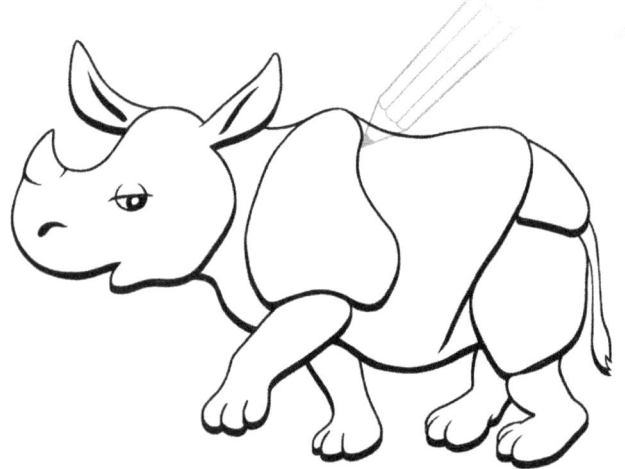

STEP 3: Erase the circles

STEP 4 – FINISH:
Add details, Draw dark

DRAWING TIPS:

Try drawing some lines thick,
and other lines thin.

Try drawing different shaped eyes

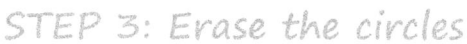 or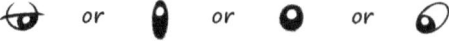

Javan Rhinoceros

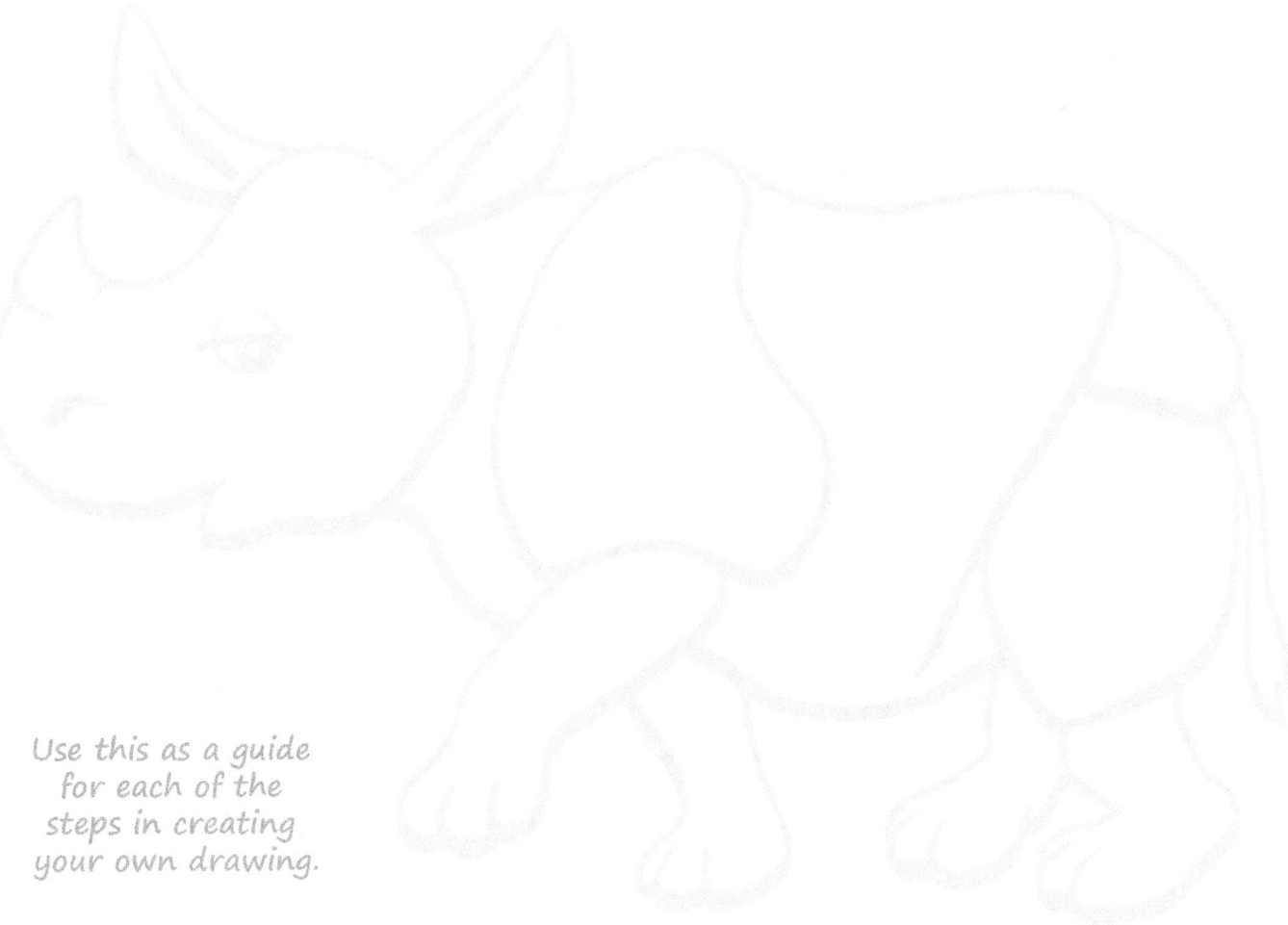

Use this as a guide
for each of the
steps in creating
your own drawing.

Fun Facts:

Javan Rhinoceros

Reasons for Endangerment:
1. Habitat Loss: Their forest homes are being cut down for farming or to use the land for other things, leaving them with fewer places to live.
2. Poaching: Even though it's illegal, some people hunt them for their horns, which are wrongly believed to have special powers.
3. Low Genetic Diversity: There are so few left that it's hard for them to have healthy babies, which makes it even harder for their population to grow.

Population in the Wild:
• Very few, around 72 known to exist in the wild as of the latest counts.

Population in Captivity:
• None are known to be kept in captivity; they live only in their natural habitat.

Countries/Areas of Natural Habitat:
• Now found only in Ujung Kulon National Park in Java, Indonesia.

Interesting Facts:
1. Shy and Solitary: They are very private animals and prefer to live alone, only coming together sometimes to mate or share a good place to eat or take a bath.
2. Love for Mud: They enjoy taking mud baths, which helps to cool them off and protect their skin from the sun and bugs.
3. Unique Folds: They have deep folds in their skin that make them look like they are wearing armor. This, along with their prehistoric look, makes them unique among animals.

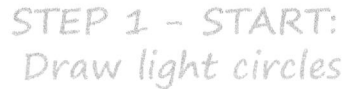

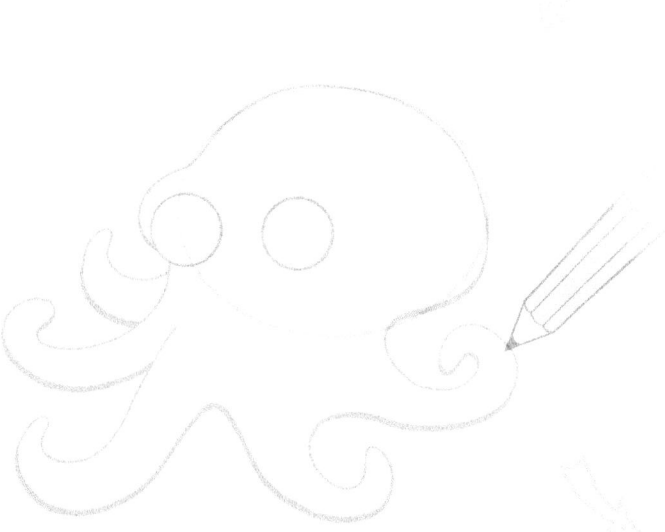

STEP 2: Draw light lines

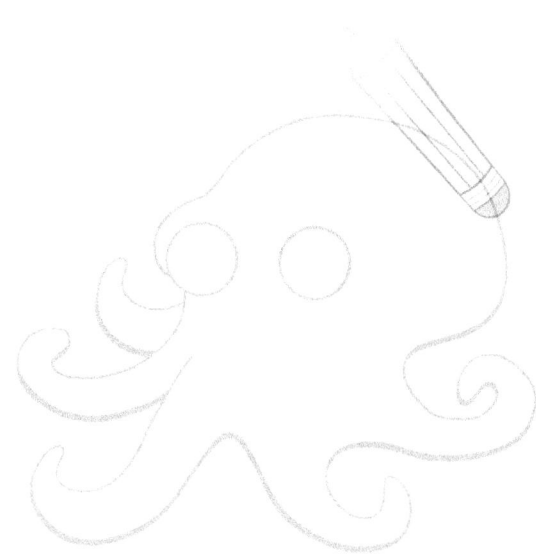

STEP 3: Erase the circles

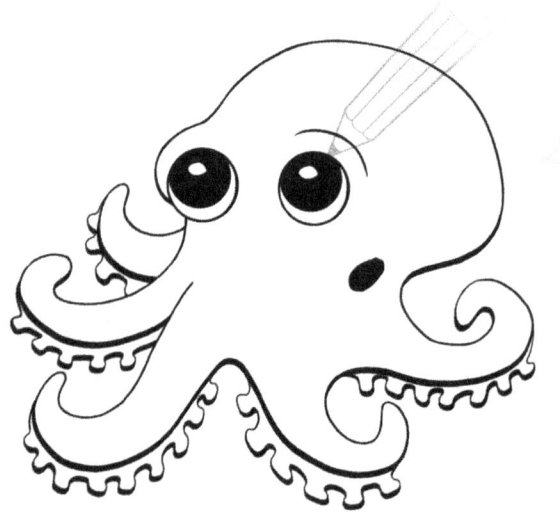

STEP 4 – FINISH:
Add details, Draw dark

DRAWING TIPS:

Try drawing some lines thick,
and other lines thin.

Try drawing different shaped eyes

  or

Cirroctopus Hochbergi Octopus

Use this as a guide
for each of the
steps in creating
your own drawing.

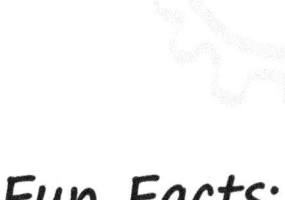

Fun Facts:

Cirroctopus Hochbergi Octopus

Reasons for Endangerment:
1. Habitat Disturbance: Their underwater homes can be disturbed by activities like fishing, trawling, or changes in the ocean environment.
2. Climate Change: Changes in ocean temperature and chemistry can affect the places where they live and find food.
3. Pollution: Water pollution can harm their health and the overall health of the ocean they live in.

Population in the Wild:
• Not well-known, as these octopuses live in deep waters and are hard to study, but they are considered to be rare.

Population in Captivity:
• Very rare in captivity due to their specific and hard-to-replicate deep-sea living conditions.

Countries/Areas of Natural Habitat:
• Found in deep waters off the coast of New Zealand.

Interesting Facts:
1. Deep Sea Dwellers: They live in very deep waters, which makes them mysterious and not often seen by people.
2. Soft and Squishy: Like other octopuses, they don't have any bones, which allows them to squeeze into tight spaces.
3. Clever Creatures: Octopuses are known for being very smart. They can solve problems, remember solutions, and are great at camouflage!

STEP 1 – START:
Draw light circles

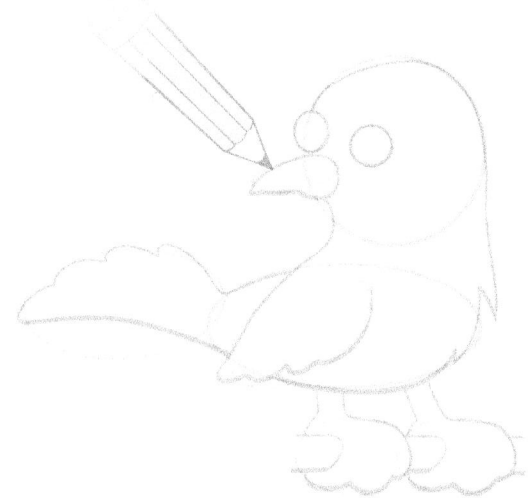

STEP 2: Draw light lines

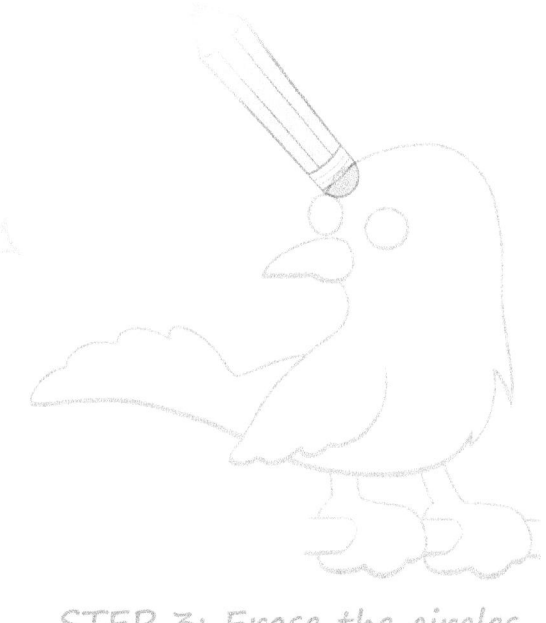

STEP 3: Erase the circles

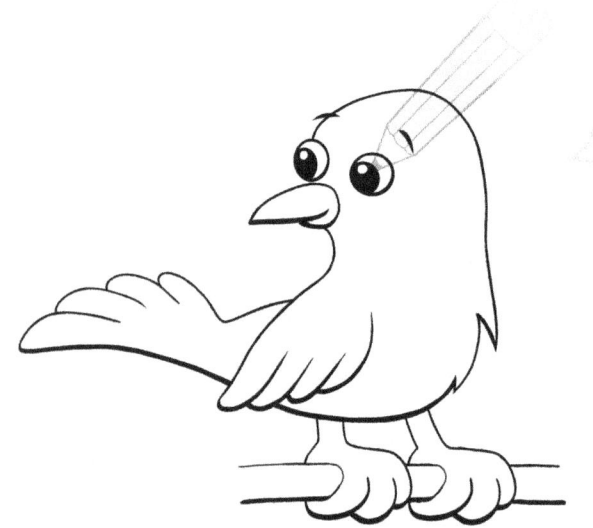

STEP 4 – FINISH:
Add details, Draw dark

DRAWING TIPS:

Try drawing some lines thick,
and other lines thin.

Try drawing different shaped eyes

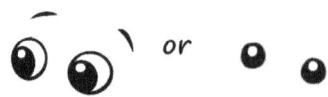 or

Pinyon Jay

Use this as a guide for each of the steps in creating your own drawing.

Fun Facts:

Pinyon Jay

Reasons for Endangerment:
1. Loss of Pinyon Pine Trees: They rely on pinyon pine trees for food, and these trees are being cut down or are dying due to disease and climate change.
2. Nesting Area Disturbance: Their nesting areas are being disrupted by human activities like building and land development.
3. Climate Change: Changes in weather patterns are affecting their habitat and the availability of their food.

Population in the Wild:
• Numbers have been decreasing, and they are considered a species of concern.

Population in Captivity:
• Not commonly found in captivity, mainly living in the wild.

Countries/Areas of Natural Habitat:
• Found mostly in the southwestern United States, especially in areas with pinyon-juniper forests.

Interesting Facts:
1. Social Birds: They are known for being very social and often travel in large groups called flocks.
2. Planting Trees: They help plant pinyon pine trees! They bury pine nuts to eat later, but some of these nuts grow into new trees.
3. Chatty Creatures: They have a wide range of calls and noises to communicate with each other, especially when warning about danger or finding food.

STEP 1 – START:
Draw light circles

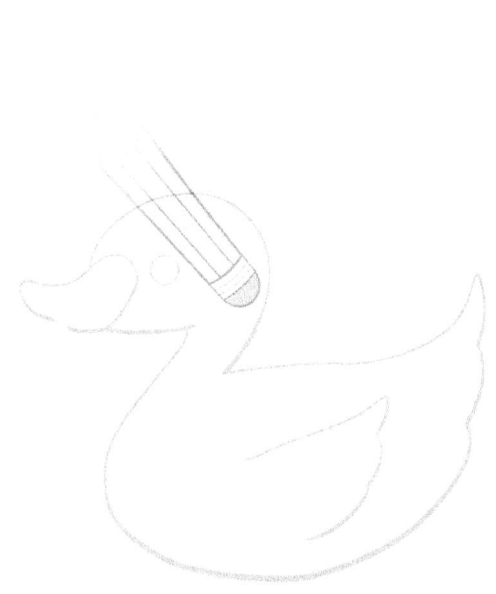

STEP 2: Draw light lines

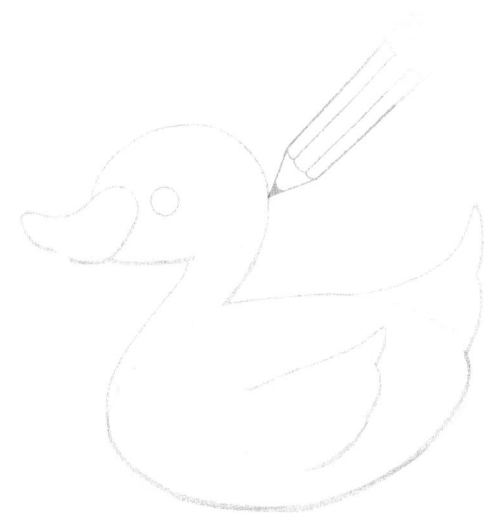

STEP 3: Erase the circles

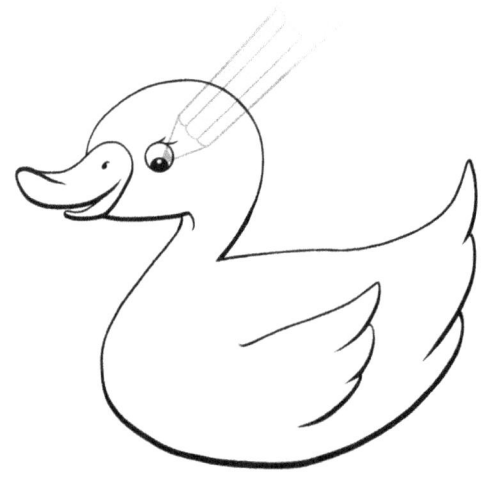

STEP 4 – FINISH:
Add details, Draw dark

DRAWING TIPS:

Try drawing some lines thick,
and other lines thin.

Try drawing different shaped eyes

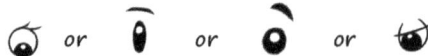 or

Madagascar Pochard Duck

Use this as a guide for each of the steps in creating your own drawing.

Fun Facts:

Madagascar Pochard Duck

Reasons for Endangerment:
1. Loss of Wetlands: Their home in the wetlands and lakes is disappearing due to land being used for farming and other human activities.
2. Water Pollution: The water where they live can get dirty from things like oil, chemicals, and trash, making it hard for them to find clean food and water.
3. Invasive Species: Animals and plants that aren't from Madagascar can move into their home, take over, and make it hard for the ducks to live.

Population in the Wild:
• Very few, only about 60 known to exist in the wild as of recent counts.

Population in Captivity:
• Around 100, with efforts to breed and eventually reintroduce them to their natural habitat.

Countries/Areas of Natural Habitat:
• Found only in Madagascar, mainly in the northern part of the island.

Interesting Facts:
1. Super Divers: They're diving ducks, which means they like to dive underwater to find their food.
2. Rare Find: They were thought to be extinct until a small group was discovered in 2006.
3. Conservation Efforts: Lots of people are working hard to protect these ducks, including setting up special areas where they can live safely and have enough food.

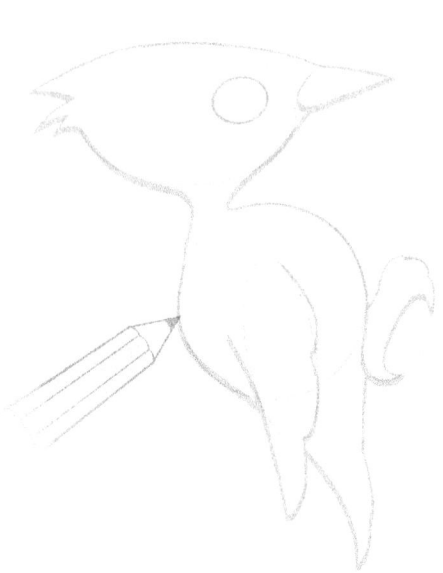

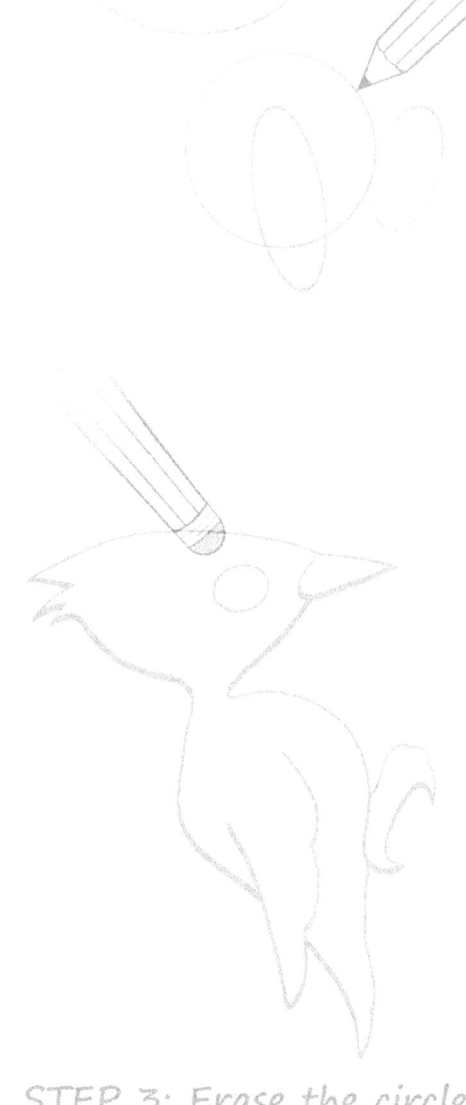

STEP 2: Draw light lines

STEP 3: Erase the circles

DRAWING TIPS:

Try drawing some lines thick,
and other lines thin.

Try drawing different shaped eyes

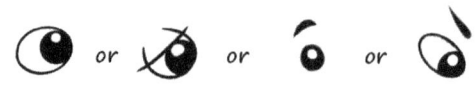

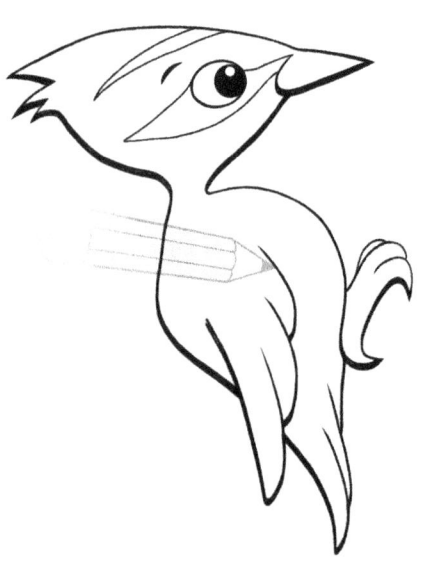

STEP 4 - FINISH:
Add details, Draw dark

Ivory-Billed Woodpecker

Use this as a guide
for each of the
steps in creating
your own drawing.

Fun Facts:

Ivory-Billed Woodpecker

Reasons for Endangerment:
   1. Habitat Loss: Their homes in large, old forests have been cut down for wood or to clear land for other uses.
   2. Hunting: They were hunted in the past for their feathers and because people thought they were harmful to trees.
   3. Competition for Nesting Holes: They need large, old trees to make their nests, but these trees are often taken by other animals or cut down.
Population in the Wild:
   • Believed to be very few, if any. This bird is so rare that some people think it might be extinct, but others still hope it's out there.
Population in Captivity:
   • None, as it has never been successfully kept in captivity.
Countries/Areas of Natural Habitat:
   • Used to be found in the southeastern United States and parts of Cuba.
Interesting Facts:
   1. Ghost Bird: It's sometimes called the "Ghost Bird" because it's so rare and hard to find.
   2. Powerful Bill: They have a strong, ivory-colored bill which they use to peck into trees to find insects to eat.
   3. Distinctive Sound: They make a unique, high-pitched sound, and the sound of their pecking is very loud, as if a large person were hammering on wood.

STEP 1 – START:
Draw light circles

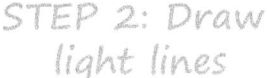

STEP 2: Draw
light lines

STEP 3: Erase
the circles

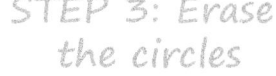

STEP 4 – FINISH:
Add details, Draw dark

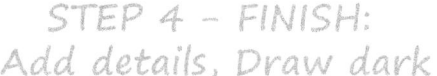

DRAWING TIPS:

Try drawing some lines thick,
and other lines thin.

Try drawing different shaped eyes

👁 or 👁 or 👁 or 👁

Ridgway's Hawk

Use this as a guide for each of the steps in creating your own drawing.

Fun Facts:

Ridgway's Hawk

Reasons for Endangerment:
1. Habitat Loss: The forests where they live are being cut down for farming and to make room for houses.
2. Pesticides: Chemicals used to kill bugs on farms can also poison these birds if they eat contaminated food.
3. Misunderstanding: Sometimes people hurt them because they think the hawks are a danger to their farm animals or pets.

Population in the Wild:
• Very few, estimated to be around 300 to 400 in the wild.

Population in Captivity:
• Some are kept in breeding programs to help increase their numbers and eventually release them back into the wild.

Countries/Areas of Natural Habitat:
• Only found in the Dominican Republic, mainly in the Los Haitises National Park and Punta Cana region.

Interesting Facts:
1. Fast Flyers: They are very skilled at flying fast and low through the forests, dodging trees while hunting for food.
2. Family Life: They like to stick together as a family. The parents and even older siblings help take care of the baby hawks.
3. Helpful Hunters: They eat rodents and insects, which helps control the population of these animals and keeps the environment balanced.

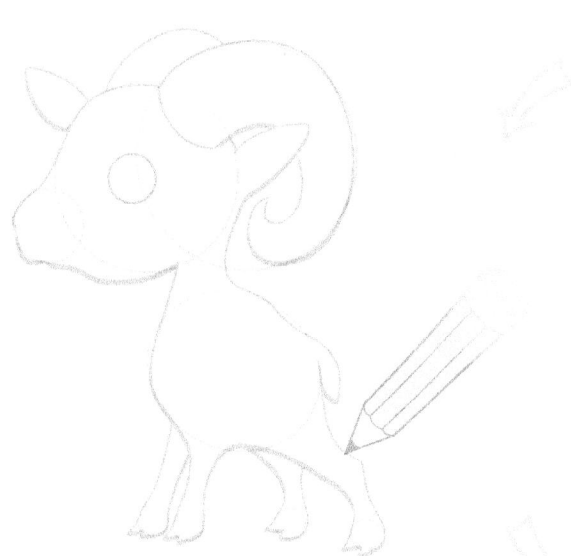

STEP 2: Draw light lines

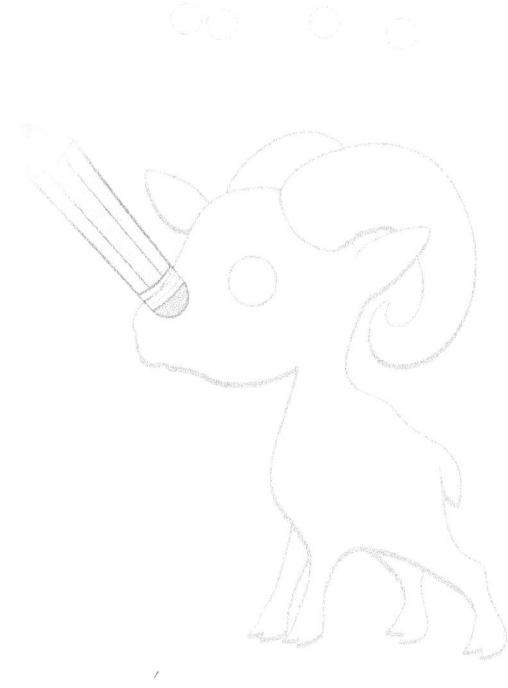

STEP 3: Erase the circles

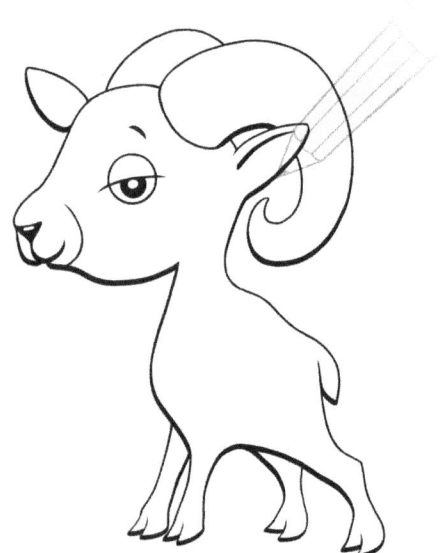

STEP 4 – FINISH:
Add details, Draw dark

DRAWING TIPS:

Try drawing some lines thick,
and other lines thin.

Try drawing different shaped eyes

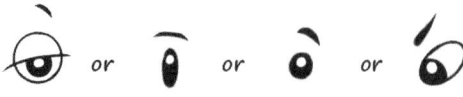 or   or   or

Peninsular Bighorn Sheep

Use this as a guide
for each of the
steps in creating
your own drawing.

Fun Facts:

Peninsular Bighorn Sheep

Reasons for Endangerment:
1. Habitat Loss: Their mountain home is being changed into land for houses and roads, making it hard for them to find food and water.
2. Disease: Diseases from domestic animals like sheep and goats can spread to them and make them sick.
3. Predators and Human Disturbance: They have to watch out for predators, and sometimes people getting too close can scare them and make it hard for them to live peacefully.

Population in the Wild:
• Around 950, but their numbers have been going up and down over the years.

Population in Captivity:
• Not typically found in captivity as they thrive best in their natural, wild environments.

Countries/Areas of Natural Habitat:
• Found in the desert mountains of southern California and Baja California in Mexico.

Interesting Facts:
1. Impressive Horns: Both males and females have big, curled horns, but the males' horns are much larger and can be used to show off during fights.
2. Amazing Climbers: They are excellent at climbing steep and rocky mountainsides to escape predators and find food.
3. Group Life: They usually live in groups, with females and young ones staying together and males forming separate groups or living alone.

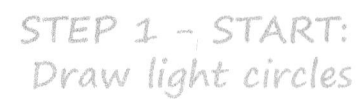

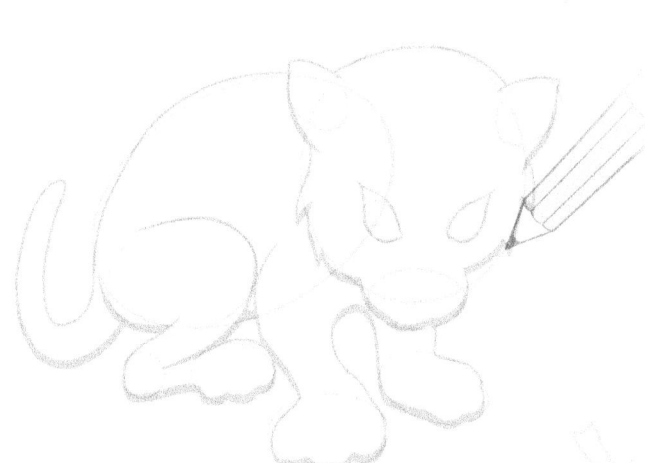

STEP 2: Draw light lines

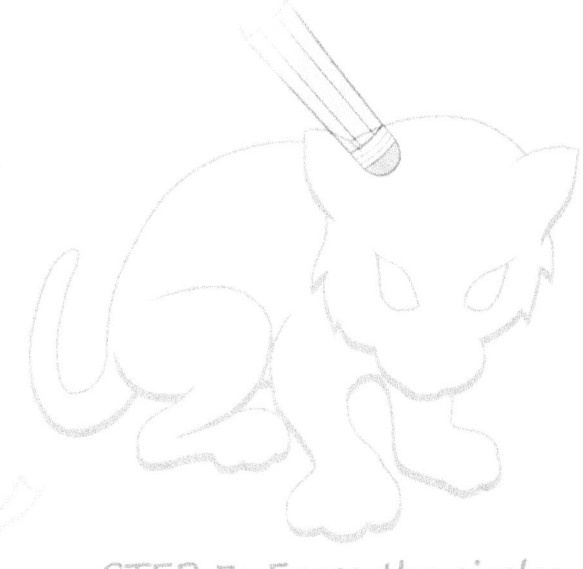

STEP 3: Erase the circles

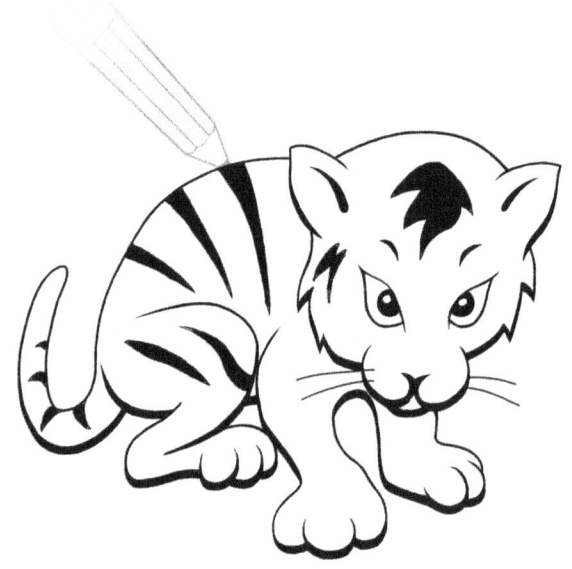

STEP 4 – FINISH:
Add details, Draw dark

DRAWING TIPS:

Try drawing some lines thick,
and other lines thin.

Try drawing different shaped eyes

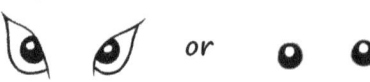 or

Sunda Tiger

Use this as a guide
for each of the
steps in creating
your own drawing.

Fun Facts:

Sunda Tiger (also known as the Sumatran Tiger)

Reasons for Endangerment:
  1. Habitat Loss: Their homes in the forests are being cut down to make room for things like palm oil plantations and other human activities.
  2. Poaching: Some people illegally hunt them for their fur or other body parts, which are used in traditional medicines.
  3. Human-Tiger Conflict: As their living space gets smaller, they sometimes come into contact with people, leading to conflicts.
Population in the Wild:
  • Very few, around 400-500 left in the wild as of the latest estimates.
Population in Captivity:
  • Several hundred in zoos around the world, where they are part of international breeding programs.
Countries/Areas of Natural Habitat:
  • Found only on the island of Sumatra in Indonesia, in habitats ranging from lowland forests to mountain forests.
Interesting Facts:
  1. Swimming Skills: Unlike many big cats, Sunda tigers are excellent swimmers and often cool off in ponds and streams.
  2. Unique Stripes: Each tiger has a unique pattern of stripes, just like humans have unique fingerprints.
  3. Nighttime Hunters: They are mostly nocturnal, meaning they are most active at night, using their excellent vision and hearing to hunt.

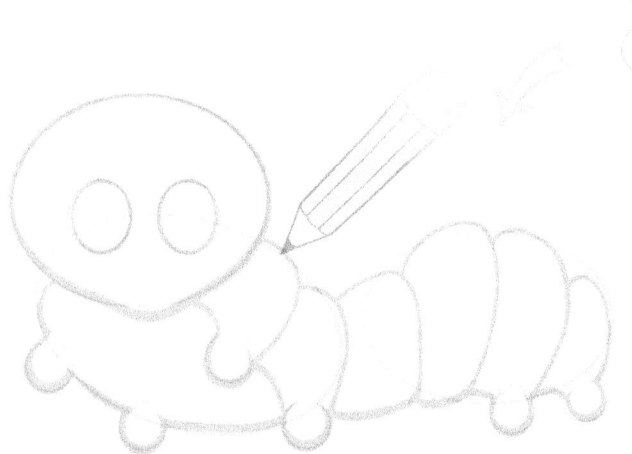

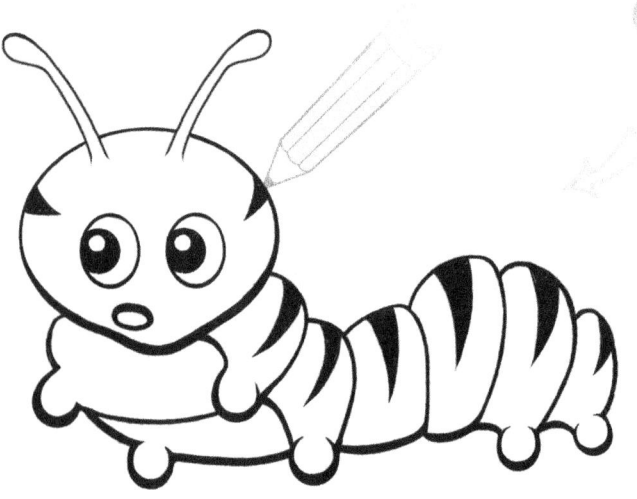

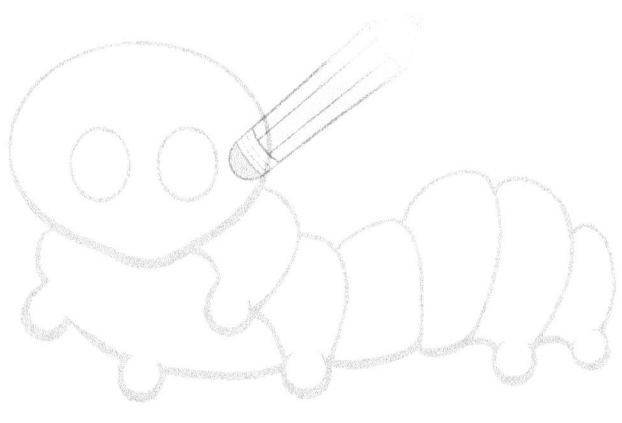

STEP 3: Erase the circles

DRAWING TIPS:

Try drawing some lines thick,
and other lines thin.

Try drawing different shaped eyes

STEP 4 - FINISH:
Add details, Draw dark

  or

Monarch Caterpillar

Use this as a guide for each of the steps in creating your own drawing.

Fun Facts:

Monarch Caterpillar and Butterfly

Reasons for Endangerment:
1. Loss of Milkweed: Their caterpillars only eat milkweed plants, and these plants are becoming rare due to land being used for farming and cities.
2. Climate Change: Changes in weather can make their long migration tough and affect the places where they lay their eggs.
3. Pesticides: Chemicals used to keep bugs away from crops can also harm monarch butterflies.

Population in the Wild:
• Numbers are decreasing, but there are still millions that migrate every year.

Population in Captivity:
• Sometimes raised in schools or homes for education, but mostly live in the wild.

Countries/Areas of Natural Habitat:
• Found across North America, especially famous for migrating from the United States and Canada to Mexico in the winter.

Interesting Facts:
1. Amazing Migrators: They travel thousands of miles in a massive group from North America to Mexico each year, one of the longest migrations of any insect!
2. Bright Warning: Their bright colors tell birds and other animals that they don't taste good, helping to protect them.
3. Four Life Stages: They go through four stages: egg, caterpillar, cocoon (chrysalis), and butterfly, changing completely at each stage.

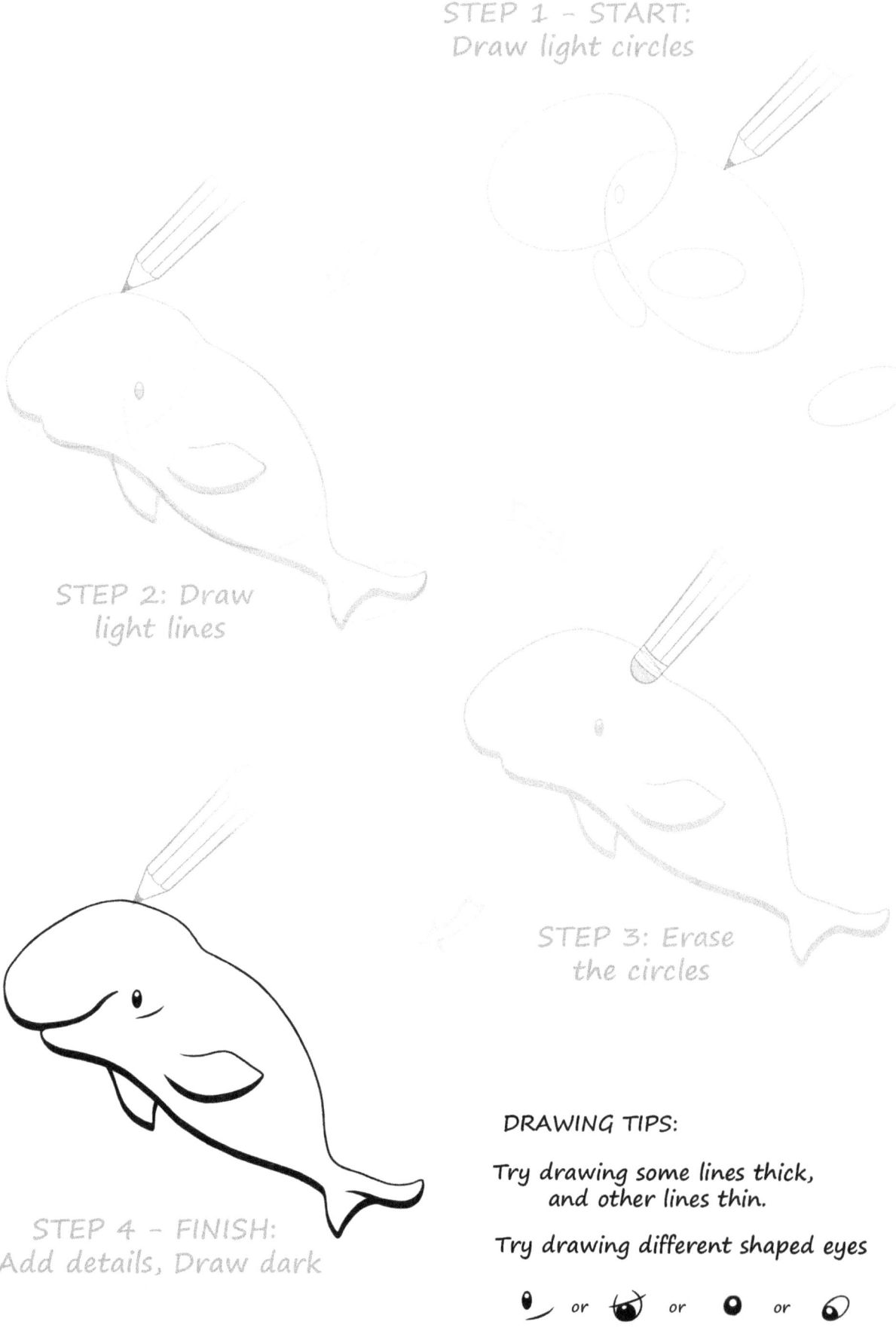

STEP 1 – START:
Draw light circles

STEP 2: Draw
light lines

STEP 3: Erase
the circles

STEP 4 – FINISH:
Add details, Draw dark

DRAWING TIPS:

Try drawing some lines thick,
and other lines thin.

Try drawing different shaped eyes

or   or   or

Baluga Whale

Use this as a guide for each of the steps in creating your own drawing.

Fun Facts:

Beluga Whale

Reasons for Endangerment:
1. Climate Change: The ice in the Arctic, where they live, is melting, which affects their habitat and the availability of their food.
2. Pollution: The water they live in can get polluted with chemicals and plastics, which can make them sick.
3. Hunting and Fishing Activities: They sometimes get caught accidentally in fishing nets, and in some areas, they are still hunted.

Population in the Wild:
• Estimated to be around 150,000, but certain populations are at risk and decreasing in number.

Population in Captivity:
• A number of them are kept in aquariums and marine parks worldwide, where they are popular with visitors.

Countries/Areas of Natural Habitat:
• Mostly found in the Arctic and sub-Arctic regions, particularly around Russia, Greenland, and North America.

Interesting Facts:
1. Canaries of the Sea: Known for their wide range of vocal sounds, they are sometimes called "canaries of the sea."
2. Incredible Neck: Unlike most other whales, they can move their necks because their cervical vertebrae are not fused.
3. Changing Color: Baby beluga whales are born gray, but as they get older, they turn white, which helps them blend in with the Arctic ice.

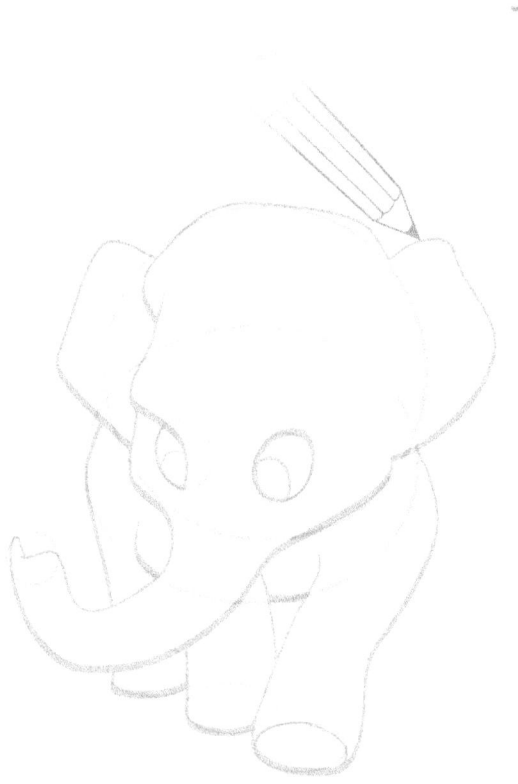

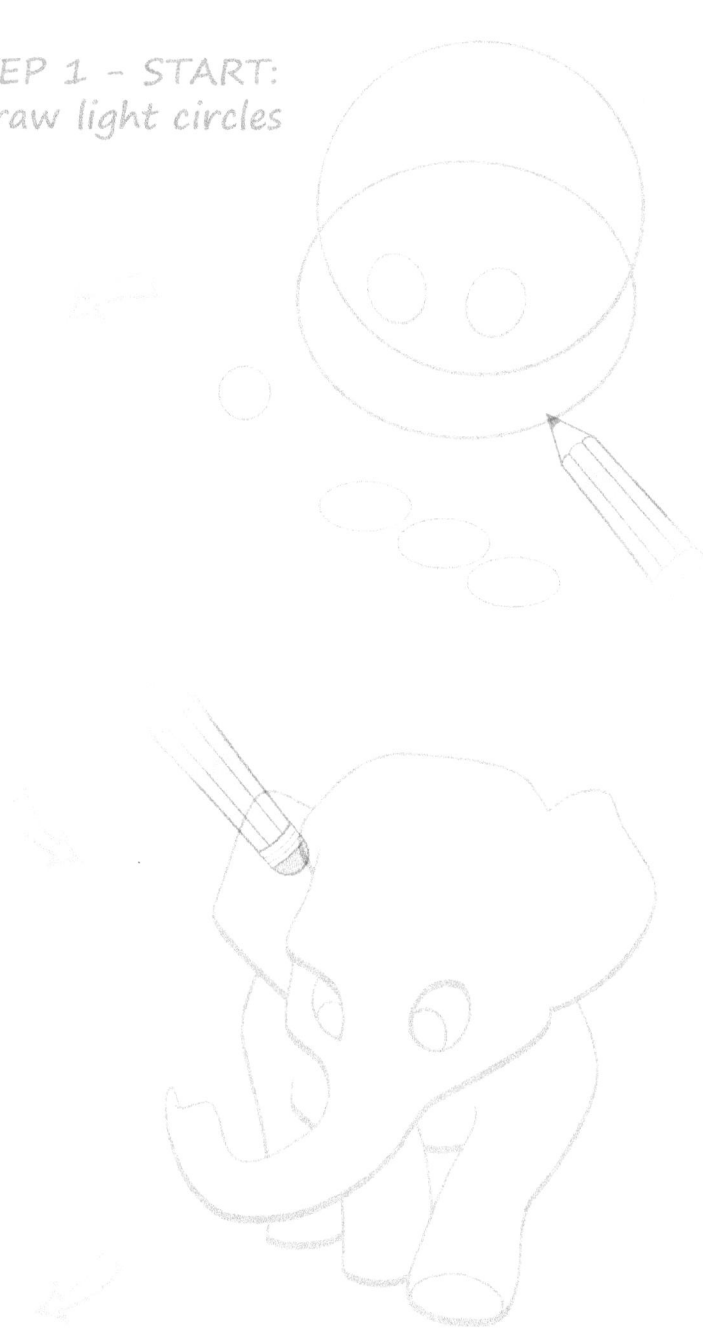

STEP 3: Erase the circles

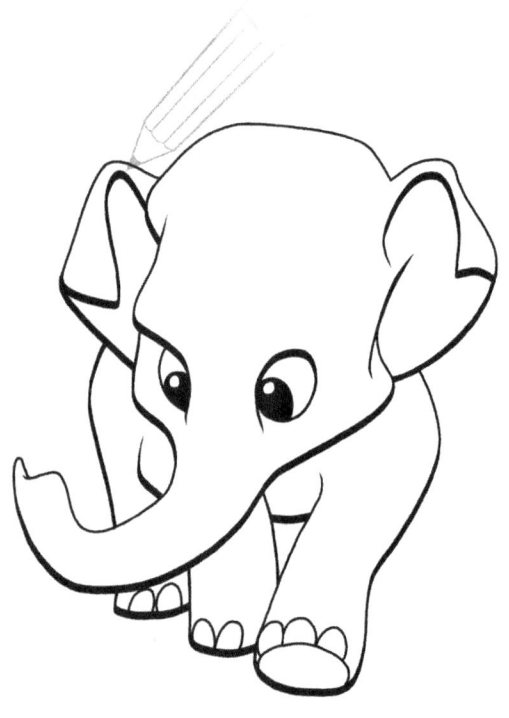

STEP 4 – FINISH:
Add details, Draw dark

DRAWING TIPS:

Try drawing some lines thick,
and other lines thin.

Try drawing different shaped eyes

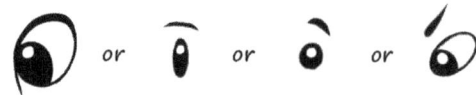

Baby Asian Elephant

Use this as a guide for each of the steps in creating your own drawing.

Fun Facts:

Asian Elephant

Reasons for Endangerment:
1. Habitat Loss: Their forest homes are being cut down for farming or to use the wood, leaving them with less space to live.
2. Human-Elephant Conflict: As their space gets smaller, they sometimes wander into farms or villages looking for food, which can lead to problems with people.
3. Poaching: Some people hunt them for their ivory tusks, even though it's illegal.

Population in the Wild:
• Estimated to be around 40,000 to 50,000, but their numbers are decreasing.

Population in Captivity:
• Found in various places like zoos, sanctuaries, and in some areas, used for work or in cultural ceremonies.

Countries/Areas of Natural Habitat:
• Live in various parts of South and Southeast Asia, including India, Sri Lanka, Thailand, and Indonesia, usually in forests.

Interesting Facts:
1. Intelligent Giants: They are very smart and have a great memory. They can remember places, other elephants, and even humans.
2. Trunk Talk: Their trunk is super versatile, used for smelling, breathing, trumpeting, drinking, and grabbing things, especially their favorite food.
3. Close Families: They live in close-knit family groups led by the oldest female, known as the matriarch.